The History of English Setter Showdogs in America

The story of the greatest English Setter showdogs in AKC history

by
Craig S. Sparkes

Published by Doral Publishing, Phoenix, Arizona
Printed in the United States of America

Interior design: The Printed Page
Cover concept: Angelika Sparkes: *Group 1 Communications*
Cover photograph: Ch. Silvermine Wagabond, courtesy of Virginia Tuck Hall
Cover design: 1106 Design
Copyedited by Jennifer Bach

Back cover photograph from the first postcard used for the campaign of an English Setter, Ch. Ludar of Blue Bar. It emphasized the distinctive pawprint marking on his muzzle. Courtesy of Bill Sears, owner of Ludar of Blue Bar and co-owner of Ben-Dar Setters.

ISBN: 0-944875-81-5
Library of Congress number: 2003107751

Foreword

*P*ersonal correspondence from the 1960s between C. A. Binney, the secretary of The Kennel Club, England, and Australian-American writer and judge Mrs. C. Bede Maxwell frequently bemoans the fact "that dog authors, on both sides of the pond and particularly in the past, had copied each other's works" without engaging in "the rigours of original research." Further, Binney and Maxwell indict the dog fancy for believing and promulgating "the scraps of dog lore as truth only because it has often appeared in print." In other words, the fancy has too often accepted dog information, anecdotes, and show records without proof, citation, qualifiers, or the establishment of criteria.

Oh, these sages of our sport now long gone from us would be wonderfully pleased to see *The History of English Setter Showdogs in America* by Craig S. Sparkes. For in this new book on English Setters the author carefully establishes a method of inquiry by which to determine which dogs and bitches have come to the fore. By explaining this in the introduction, the author demonstrates from the outset that the dogs presented in prose and in pose are there because they meet the criteria, and not for any other reason. Craig Sparkes has undertaken a formidable task in gathering data on the winning English of the twentieth century and especially in researching the early years of the century. His sources include American Kennel Club records, *Popular Dogs Magazine, The Gazette*, published interviews of breeders and judges of the era, export records from England and Scotland, and published kennel advertising. The kennels that exported foundation stock to the new breeders in the United States are identified, and the early kennels that produced the show winners are named along with the owners.

Yet this is far from a collection of facts and show records. It includes quotations from Earl Kruger about the magnificence of Mallhawk Jeff, the words of C. N. Myers, the press reports of a fight in the Best in Show ring when Maro of Maridor stood his ground against the Dane, and analysis showing that according to AKC Best in Show records, half of the top ten English Setters won between 1932 and 1950. In addition, this book tells of the period of English Setter history that to date no book has included. It describes the beginnings of the English Setter Association of America, where it held its first Specialty, and what dogs won the early Futurities. Perhaps most interesting of all, and for the first time, this book identifies the three sets of top-of-the-chart winning brothers.

Over one hundred photographs, many of which have not been published in over fifty years and some of which have never been published, form a visual continuum of the great strength and enduring quality of the breed. While those who are able to see only the superficiality of modern coat, trimming, and exaggerated show poses may miss the excellence of the great dogs of the past, knowledgeable students of the breed will find new appreciation for the tenets of type—the paradigm of excellence that has long been with us.

This book provides interesting comparisons and contrasts over time between English Setters and top winners from other breeds. The analysis of show statistics tells how this breed fared on the all-breed charts of wining show dogs. And the time span of this history includes one hundred years of the twentieth century. Interviews with English Setter breeders, judges, and handlers breathe life into the fascinating records of modern times. The role of handlers and owner-handlers is included. The Appendixes have lists and charts for quick reference, and the bibliography provides a valuable starting point for new research.

No author works alone, and Craig Sparkes has chosen to consult some of the most knowledgeable dog people of the day. They have provided descriptions of the great dogs, kennels, and shows from firsthand experience. And other consultants helped provide avenues into archives both public and private. This *History of English Setter Showdogs in America* is the first book devoted to the reporting and analyzing of English Setters in competition. It is also the first book since 1982 that has chronicled the breed in terms of Davis Tuck's concept of the "winning strain." This book about winners is a winner.

Craig Sparkes is no stranger to winning English Setters. He has bred them, handled them, chauffeured them, carried their gear, picked up after them, and paid their way in the world. Most of all he has loved them, and he continues to have a "Goodtime" doing just that. Born and raised in Chicago, Craig began his academic career in religious studies until he fell in love with Angelika and rock 'n' roll. The leader of a successful rock band, Craig was a singer and guitarist for several years until the draft and the Vietnam War abruptly ended his rise in the entertainment field. Leaving the United States Army as a first lieutenant, Craig returned to college as a business major. With an MBA in finance from the University of Chicago, he entered the field of banking and in 1977 moved to the Bay Area in California. Presently, he is an entrepreneur in technology start-up firms.

Craig and Angie Sparkes began their interest in Setters in 1974 with Ch. Popkins Goodtime, first in a line of winners for the kennel under whose banner Ch. Goodtime's Silk Teddy reigned supreme— becoming the top-winning bitch in English Setter history. Serving as National Specialty show chairman and vice-president at large of the English Setter Association of America, Craig has also served as an officer in the Western English Setter Club and was president of the Golden Gate English Setter Club.

It is my honor to introduce this fascinating book and to introduce the author, my friend of many years, Craig S. Sparkes. He has uncovered vital information that had been lost to the breed's archives, and he has conducted an inquiry into age-old statements of common acceptance; using painstaking research, he has disproved many former pet shibboleths that had long passed for truth.

Marsha Hall Brown
Stone Gables English Setters

Dedication

This book is dedicated to Angelika Sparkes, my wife, my love, my companion, my business partner, who shares my experiences with that most gentle of man's best friends, the English Setter.

Angie encouraged me to write this book and was my most ardent supporter during my research. Angie was the one who introduced me to these magnificent creatures, and we made them part of our lives. She shared with me her incredible knowledge and understanding of the breed, and through her Setters made me part of the dog show world with all its wonderment, joy, excitement, and triumph. Angie has always made me a better man.

I hope that those who read my work will find that same understanding and sense of wonderment that Angie and her Setters have instilled in me.

Craig S. Sparkes
Martinez, California
2002

Acknowledgments

One person alone cannot accomplish writing a book that traces history over a one-hundred-year period. There were many, many English Setter fanciers and dog world luminaries who contributed their archives, photographs, and memories to my project. Without them this work could not have happened. I wish to thank all of them for their time, efforts, and friendship.

First, to *Marsha Hall Brown*, my friend and mentor. Marsha inspired me to write this book and has been a constant source of information, contacts, and advice. As an English Setter breeder, junior handler, AKC judge, and accomplished author, Marsha has been gracious and kind enough to share with me her experiences and knowledge. Marsha opened her home and library to me, and I thank her for the countless hours I spent reading, copying, and reviewing a wealth of historical information. Her photographs and slide collection yielded many prints never before seen, and her portrait of the great Ch. Blue Dan of Happy Valley has added immensely to the illustrations in this book. She has made me a far better author than I thought I could be.

To *Dr. Alvin Grossman*, breeder of champion American Cockers, AKC judge, and publisher. Over the years, as this book took shape in my mind, Dr. Grossman would always say, "When you're ready, call me." When I finally was ready, he was true to his word and took on my project. Dr. Grossman made my project a reality.

To *Davis Tuck*, a man I never had the privilege to know and the author of the definitive book on English Setters, *The Complete English Setter*. His text, first published in 1951, has been the "bible" for every serious student of the breed. The information, recommendations, guidelines, and photographs are as relevant today as they were fifty years ago. His book needs to be read again and again. Each time, the true meaning or significance of another part is made clear. Davis Tuck made me want to add to his efforts.

To *Virginia Tuck Hall*, a most gracious and generous woman. Virginia Tuck was an accomplished handler, master groomer, and renowned AKC judge as well as the wife of Davis Tuck. It was Virginia who typed the original manuscript of his book. I thank her for her insights and memories of the great Setters of the '40s, '50s, and more. She shared these with me and helped me better understand Setters and the men and women who showed them. Virginia's kindness and generosity made a link to the efforts of her husband and added encouragement for my efforts.

To a truly remarkable trio: *Anne Rogers Clark, Jane Kamp Forsyth, and Robert Forsyth.* These three were the consummate handlers of their day and had, and still have, a significant influence on many of the professional handlers we know today. Their impact on the breed and the sport as handlers and judges cannot be overstated. They graciously gave of their time to talk with me about their experiences and the handlers and the Setters they had known, shown, and judged. They provided the first-person stories so important in a historical text such as this. I am honored they talked with me and truly grateful for the insight they brought to my work.

To *Bill and Lovey Trotter*, English Setter breeders and AKC judges, for sharing with me their experiences and archives of the post-World War II era of English Setters. The Trotters knew the great C. N. Myers of Blue Bar fame and Bill Holt of Rock Falls fame. They bred National Specialty-winning dogs and judged some of the past greats. They have literally seen and done it all, and I thank them for all their considerations.

To *Geraldine Hayes*, historian/archivist; *Barbara Kolk*, librarian; and *Ann Sergi*, assistant librarian, at the AKC Library in New York. These generous and infinitely patient women were of invaluable assistance in researching some of the data critical to this book. Geraldine is also the historian for the Morris & Essex KC and provided valuable contacts for my efforts. Ann researched all the Westminster Group placements, and Barbara forwarded her notes and research assistance. Thanks to these ladies, my work contains more data and important information than would otherwise have been possible.

To *Meg M. Stuble*, VP of operations, St. Hubert's Giralda, for sending me never-before-seen photos from the great Morris & Essex KC shows. Meg provided an important historical link to the earliest of English Setter winners at Morris & Essex. She searched the archives of St. Hubert's and made copies of the photographs that appear in this book. I am truly in her debt.

To *Corky Vroom*, professional handler extraordinaire. Corky has been my friend, handler, and competitor for more than twenty years. One of the last all-breed handlers licensed by the AKC, Corky has been a member of the PHA since 1966 and is the current president of that body. He apprenticed under the great Harry Sangster and has piloted some of the greatest dogs in AKC history. Corky provided the link between the great handlers of the '50s and '60s and the ones I have seen. His cooperation was the inspiration for the chapter on handlers in this book.

To *Dick Fox*, English Setter breeder and AKC judge, for his gracious assistance in researching pedigrees and other historical facts. Dick was my "special researcher" at the AKC Library in New York and selflessly spent days and weeks researching a seemingly endless series of questions. Dick Fox provided his meticulously researched data on the top-producing English Setter sires and dams. His work adds immeasurably to my own research, and his efforts allowed me to complete my project.

To *Dr. Carl Sillman*, ESAA historian, English Setter fancier, and researcher. Carl is researching and preparing material for a history of the famous Blue Bar Kennels of Clinton N. Myers. His collections of old *AKC Gazettes, Popular Dogs,* and detailed ESAA National Specialty information from the Blue Bar era (1934-58) provided valuable data for this book.

To *Garth Gourlay*, Canadian English Setter breeder and photographer for English Setter Association of America National Specialties for more than a decade, for providing his photograph collection for use in this book. Garth had photos from the earliest days of English Setter activity, and his generosity is most appreciated.

To *Thomas Hall*, editor extraordinaire. Thomas spent countless hours reviewing my manuscript and turning my thoughts and words into proper grammar and prose. His advice and patience helped me weave the thoughts and data into the story I was trying to tell. This is the only part of the book that Thomas has not touched. In between his editing of serious religious works, Tom would encourage me to rise to levels of literature that I never knew I could reach. He made me a better writer, and I'm in his debt.

A special thanks for all those whose friendship and contributions to my "historical collection" over the past fifteen years served as the basis for this effort. They include:

- Rebec Pusey Riggs (Cabin Hill)
- Sally & Dick Howe (Clariho)
- Ray and Barbara Parsons (Raybar)
- The estate of Irene Castle Phillips Khatoonian Schlintz (the Phillips System)
- M. A. Samuelson (Heathrow)
- Howard Nugood, chairman of the Morris & Essex KC Historical Committee

Finally, to all the English Setters we've owned: the great, near-great, and those who were known only inside our homes. These majestic animals have brought me happiness and peace. They have given me unconditional love. They never had a bad day and would smile and grin, and greet me joyfully whenever I came home. They made me laugh, and I cried when they left me. Some were pure magic in the show ring and taught me what greatness was really like. Others were simple souls that taught me humility. They have made me a better human being.

Contents

*Charles Inglee & Ch. Inglehurst Reward at the 1930 Morris & Essex K.C.
(photo courtesy of St. Hubert's Animal Welfare Center, Madison N.J.)*

Introduction

The English Setter is a purposeful sporting dog, yet incredibly beautiful and athletic in its conformation and movement. As the ancient foundation stock for the Irish and Gordon Setters, English Setters possess the strength of the Gordon and the grace of the Irish with a calm and warm disposition all their own. English Setters have been among the premier breeds since the formation of the American Kennel Club (AKC); in fact, along with eight other Sporting breeds, they were among the first pure breeds accepted by the club in 1878. The dog with *AKC registration #1* was an *English Setter* named *Adonis*, owned by Mr. George Delano of New Bedford, Massachusetts, and the first AKC

The English Setter, Adonis
No. 1 of the American Kennel Club Stud Book,
published in Volume 1, 1878, of the National American Kennel Club.

show dog to amass one hundred Best in Shows was the legendary Ch. Rock Falls Colonel of the early 1950s. Furthermore, many of the greatest professional handlers are closely associated with the English Setters within their care.

This book will chronicle the AKC show history of the English Setter and describe those attributes of the English Setter that contribute to success in the ring. It is not intended to be a definitive history of the breed, but rather will focus on the bench show chronicle of these magnificent dogs. Anyone who has been to a dog show and watched or participated all the way from the Classes through the Best of Breed and on to the Best in Show judging has witnessed at first hand the excitement and beauty of show dogs in their element. Among the finest descriptions of the English Setter show dog is one written by the late Clinton N. Myers of the famous Blue Bar Kennels. C. N. Myers was one of the foremost (if not *the* foremost) American breeders of English Setters, who in the 1930s acquired some of the finest English Setters as foundation stock for his legendary Blue Bar line and by the 1940s had established his dogs as some of the best in the country. His article "***The English Setter as a show dog***" was part of the English Setter Association of America's official membership information guide from 1954 through the 1980s. It captures the essence the breed as experienced and defined by the man who bred more winning English Setters than anyone.

> *Watch the Sporting Group at a dog show and listen to the crowd's roar of admiration when the English Setter steps out!*

> *With proud head held high, feathers flying and gay tail swinging, he floats like a cloud in easy grace as he parades the ring. He is a dog of distinction, clothed in a coat of sparkling white flecked with orange-red or blue-black ticking.*

> *Small wonder that he is a crowd pleaser, that judges so often give first prize among sporting dogs and the most coveted of all awards—"Best Dog in Show." Of the three leading Best in Show winners in the long history of the*

American Kennel Club, two have been English Setters: Ch. Maro of Maridor and Ch. Rock Falls Colonel. English Setters have won the top prize at the largest dog shows in America—the Westminster Kennel Club held in New York's Madison Square Garden and the great Morris and Essex Kennel Club in Madison N.J.

The great beauty of this breed is natural too. An English Setter requires no alteration of his anatomy. His ears, tail, and other parts are left as Nature made them. Even his coat needs relatively little trimming or clipping for the neat picture show dogs must present.

The English Setter trains easily for show work. His ever-present desire to please serves him well in learning the intricacies of show-ring etiquette. His constancy insures that he will always give "a good show."

And at the show he is a pleasure to handle. Whether you keep him in a crate (a sanctuary he dearly loves) or on the bench provided by the show superintendent, he is quiet and at peace with man and other dogs.

But most satisfying of all his attributes as the ideal show dog is the English Setter's own enjoyment of his role in the ring. For him, it's fun to stand still as a statue while the judge considers his points. And when he is called upon to display his gaiting action, a glad light comes to his eyes; he trots with spectacular flair, always watching his handler for the slightest command of leash or voice.

Every English Setter is a winner at heart, a champion in spirit.

I first read those words in the early 1970s and knew I had to own such magnificent dogs. Thirty years later they have enriched my life, and C. N. Myers' words echo in my mind when I look across the show ring.

Ch. Stagedoor Penny Lane

(photo from Joan Savage collection)

It is not enough merely to record which dogs won what ribbons. The research into the dogs mentioned in this book includes articles from the leading dog publications of each era in an attempt to recapture a sense of the actual performance of these dogs at the shows to suggest the vitality and spirit that made them great. In addition, first-hand accounts and anecdotes from leading figures in the English Setter world will help portray the individual and everyday nature of these winning dogs.

A study of the photographs included in this book will show that from the first great English Setter show dogs to the present-day champions, the breed has changed little. These naturally beautiful animals have been wisely bred to preserve the majesty and character of the breed for more than one hundred years. In fact, half of the top ten English Setters as measured by AKC Best in Show records were shown between 1932 and 1950. It is my hope that this book will encourage present and future English Setter breeders to cherish those qualities and continue producing excellent and exciting show dogs. With more than one hundred photographs of the greatest English

Setters in history, this book can also be a useful resource for judges in visualizing the English Setter Standard. Finally, anyone interested in dog shows and dog show history will find a remarkable collection of photographs and stories about the "winningest" English Setters.

Another aim of this book is to debunk some of the popular myths (actually excuses) about showing dogs. The most common is, "You can't compete against professional handlers." But the greatest English Setter show dog of all, Ch. Rock Falls Colonel, was owner-handled his entire career. Another fable is, "Bitches cannot compete with males." Yet the incomparable Ch. Goodtime's Silk Teddy holds the record for Sporting Group firsts with 163. She not only dominated her Sporting competition but also won a record three consecutive ESAA National Specialties, beating all comers, male or female. A similar "truism" is, "Blue Belton English Setters can't win." Still, the English Setter with the fifth all-time Best in Show record for the breed is Ch. Blue Dan of Happy Valley, who also won the first ESAA National Specialty. Finally, a "tall tale" currently making the rounds at judges seminars is, "Coloration doesn't matter," or as it is

Ch. Goodtime's Silk Teddy
(photo courtesy of Craig & Angie Sparkes – Goodtime)

sometimes expressed, "Think of them all as green".[1] If you look at the photographs of the great English Setter show dogs, however, you will see they had one thing in common: *They were beautiful to look at.* Beautifully marked, beautifully colored, in short, pleasing to the eye.

Since this is a book about English Setter show dogs, a short set of terms and definitions needs to be discussed. According to *The History of the AKC* from the club's web site, AKC-sanctioned dog shows operated under an evolving set of rules and procedures until 1923. At that time, all breeds (except those in the Miscellaneous Competition) were separated into five groups:

- Group 1–Sporting Dogs
  (which at the time included all hound breeds)
- Group 2–Working Dogs
- Group 3–Terriers
- Group 4–Toy Breeds
- Group 5–Non-Sporting Breeds

The Best of Breed winners in each Group were then judged together to determine the best dog in that Group, and finally, the five Group winners met to determine the Best dog in Show (BIS). By 1924 the new Group alignment and judging format was in general use.

Therefore, the historic English Setters mentioned and described in this book will be those shown at AKC-sanctioned dog shows beginning in 1924.

Criteria for Selection

The book chronicles the accomplishments of English Setters at AKC-sanctioned All-Breed dog shows and AKC-approved English Setter Specialty shows sponsored by the ESAA and local English Setter breed clubs of the ESAA. While many English Setters have had fine show careers and made their owners proud, a fair and logical set of criteria was needed for selection of an English Setter to this book. If a dog satisfied *any one of those criteria,* it was included in this book. The first selection criterion was whether the English Setter had won a recognized Annual Award. Over the years, various organizations have sponsored annual awards based upon some formula of dog show wins. The awards used and referenced by this book include:

- *ESAA Dog of the Year*—awarded to the English Setter defeating the most dogs as Best of Breed at AKC-sanctioned dog shows.

- *Pedigree Best Dog in Breed*—same as ESAA Dog of the Year

- *Quaker Oats Award—Sporting Group*—at one time, this award was sponsored by the Ken-L-Ration dog food division of Quaker Oats and was awarded to the dog winning the most Group firsts in each AKC Group.

- *Nature's Recipe Award—Sporting Group*—the continuation of the Quaker Oats Awards, now sponsored by Nature's Recipe Dog Food and *Dog World Magazine*. Awarded to the dog winning the most Group firsts in each AKC Group.

- *Phillips System*—An awards system, developed and tracked by the late Irene Castle Phillips Khatoonian Schlintz, which recorded the number of dogs defeated at the Breed, Group, and Best in Show levels. Dogs are ranked at the Breed, Group, and All-Breed levels based on cumulative dogs defeated. The Phillips System was published from 1956 to 1991.

- *Top 10 in Group (similar to the Phillips System)*—since the mid-'80s, several dog publications, notably *Dog News* and *Canine Chronicle*, have recorded the number of dogs defeated at the Breed, Group, and Best in Show levels. Dogs are ranked at the Group and All-Breed levels based on the cumulative number of dogs defeated.

- *All-Breed level*—same as Top 10 in Group. Currently recorded and sponsored by *Dog News*.

Two other selection criteria are based upon accomplishments in the Best in Show or Specialty ring. English Setters were included in this book if they won:

- *Five or more AKC Best in Shows (BIS)* and/or
- *Three or more Separate Specialty Best in Specialty Shows (BISS)*

Another level of achievement that indicates the mettle of a great show dog is winning at some of the most competitive and prestigious dog shows. For this book, an English Setter that won at any of the following four shows will be mentioned:

- *ESAA National Specialty*—the annual dog show, put on by the English Setter Association of America, only for English Setters. It is the premier breed-level event to win, and many of the great English have won the "National."

- *ESAA Futurity*—a special event for dogs between the ages of six months and eighteen months held in conjunction with the ESAA National Specialty. Dogs must be nominated at the time of whelp to compete. Many of the greatest English Setter show dogs have won Best in Futurity or Best of Opposite Sex in Futurity. The Futurity began in 1936 and ended during World War II in 1943. It was revived in 1976 and continues to this day.

- *Westminster Kennel Club*—one of the oldest AKC clubs in the United States. Held at Madison Square Garden in New York, the Westminster show has long been regarded as the premier U.S. dog show and was the first to award Best in Show under the 1924 AKC format. A Best of Breed win, Group Placement, or Best in Show at "The Garden" is a memorable accomplishment.

Benching area for Sporting dogs, 1934 Morris & Essex K.C.
(photo courtesy of St. Hubert's Animal Welfare Center, Madison N.J.)

■ *Morris & Essex Kennel Club*—another of the most prestigious AKC dog shows. The Morris & Essex KC held its annual show on the polo grounds of the estate of Mrs. Geraldine (Rockefeller) Dodge in Madison, New Jersey. The "old Morris and Essex" show ran from 1927 to 1957. At one time it was the largest dog show in the world, with an entry of more than four thousand. It was recently revived in 2000 and will hold its next full show in 2005. Winning the Breed, Group, or Best in Show at the "old Morris & Essex" was an accomplishment on a par with a win at Westminster.

Companion reading and reference

Although relatively few books have been written about English Setters, lovers of the breed are fortunate to have Davis Tuck's *The Complete English Setter: A Compilation of Interesting Facts, Data, and Observations on Breeding, Raising, Training, Showing, and Hunting English Setters,* long considered the "bible" for serious students of the breed. To be sure, a number of individuals have profoundly influenced English Setters through their breeding programs and show stock. People like A. J. Kruger, Eric Bergishagen, Norm McConnell, J. J. Sinclair, Dr. A. A. Mitten, and C. N. Myers made lasting contributions to the breed. Yet it was Davis Tuck (also a major contributor to English Setter stock through his Silvermine Kennels) who committed all of this knowledge to writing so that future generations would have a road map to follow. Virginia Tuck Hall, who has been an invaluable source of information for this book, presented the author with a signed first edition of her husband's book from her archives; this gift is the crowning piece of my personal library.

David Tuck was an author, engineer, inventor, farmer, and breeder of magnificent English Setters. When my wife and I first became interested in the breed in the early 1970s, we bought a copy of the third edition of Tuck's book (revised by the late Elsworth Howell) and virtually memorized its contents. We were not the only breeders of that time to do so. In an interview with *Setter's Inc.* Magazine published in the February/March 1988 issue, Neal Weinstein of Guys 'n Dolls Kennels, one of the most influential English Setter breeders of the last thirty years, responded to a question about the origins of his breeding program by saying:

> *One interesting thing that I did was I studied the English Setter book* [The Complete English Setter by Davis Tuck] *and their instructions on breeding, like I wore it out, and I tried to learn from it what to do. In looking at the pages of the book, in looking at the past dogs that were shown, I tried to pick out a dog that I would really like....It turned out to be Ch. Rock Falls Colonel.*

Davis Tuck and his wife, Virginia (Ginny), were also consummate dog show masters. No less an authority on dogs than Anne Rogers Clark recently wrote in a column titled *Annie on Sporting Dog Presentation* in the August 2001 issue of *Dogs in Review*:

> *We also learned a tremendous amount about many breeds of dogs—how they should show, how they should be conditioned, and how they should be trimmed correctly. We had old masters to learn from; some taught us, some we stole from just by watching.*
>
> *Our wonderful friends, Ginny Tuck and her husband* [Davis Tuck] *who owned Silvermine Kennels, were way ahead of their time....Ginny dried with an electric dryer with the dog on the grooming table so that every hair was laid straight and dried that way.*
>
> *Are you saying "SO WHAT?" In those days she was the ONLY person showing those breeds (English Setters and English Cockers) that did this. All others were bathed, toweled off, and had the coat straightened out. And then a large towel was pinned on them...and they were allowed to dry...!*

Davis Tuck's book was first published in 1951 and was revised three times. The first revision (the second edition) was made by Elsworth Howell and published by his company, Howell Books, in 1964. Elsworth added to the original book chapters on "Leading

Winners" and "Leading Sires and Dams." He again revised the book in 1972 (the third edition), updating his chapters. The book was last published in 1982 (the fourth edition), further revised and updated with a contribution by Judy Graef. These books can still be obtained at dog shows and through major book retailers. The reader is encouraged to consider *all* editions of Davis Tuck's book as companions to the present text. The detail and level of research he developed cannot be duplicated. Davis Tuck developed a concept he called the "winning strain." This was his characterization in 1950 of the lineage that produced the dominant breed-type show English.

Follow along as we keep track of this "winning strain" while chronicling the greats of the past and building a picture of the English Setter.

Endnotes

1. This reference, suggesting that color and markings are not important in English Setters, has been used, unfortunately, at judges workshops and seminars by those who are misstating a part of the original "standing room only" lectures by C. Bede Maxwell. Today's speakers have taken liberties and added their own conclusions that are not supported by the Standard, nor are they accurate to the source. This present-day confusion and misinformation stems from a 35-mm. color slide that showed a correct, well-made English Setter with full coat, and in show trim. However, the dog had investigated the inside of a pot filled with green paint, and the results produced a setter with green muzzle and green leg furnishings. Mrs. Maxwell *never* suggested that color and markings were not important. What she did say was that the dog in the picture was still a good dog, regardless of the day he was green. (Marsha Hall Brown, interview, December 2001.)

Imp. ENGLISH SETTER

"Mallwyd Bob"

AT STUD-- to a limited number of approved bitches --$25.00

THE PROPERTY OF

T. P. McCONNELL

VICTORIA, B. C., CANADA

"Mallwyd Bob" is a good sized blue Belton, ticked all over without patches. He has a grand body with deep chest, and profuse coat and feather, and his head is a picture. He has plenty of bone, good legs and feet and is perfectly straight "fore and aft," and a good mover. Thoroughly field broken and the sire of the sensational English winner "Brown Hill Bob" and many others.

His pedigree, as can be seen within, is irreproachable, containing all the best blood of recent years, without being too closely inbred.

Bitches for service may be shipped direct to me from outside points, but dates must be arranged for before hand, and stud fees paid at time of service. All American bitches will be cleared at customs and re-exported free of charge.

Ch. Mallwyd Bob stud advertisement circa 1904
(from the author's collection)

Chapter One

The Beginning and Early Years, 1900-30

It is generally accepted that English Setters (as a distinct breed) existed and were used for bird hunting more than four hundred years ago. We find reference to them in a 1570 book titled *Of Englishe Dogges* by John Caius, royal physician to King Edward VI, and again in an illustrated book published in 1582, *Partridge Shooting and Partridge Hawking* by Hans Bols. They probably came from crosses between the Pointer, Water Spaniel, and Spanish Spaniel. Many illustrations from that period show dogs with classic English Setter characteristics. It is interesting that in 1878 the first nine breeds recognized by the AKC as "pure bred" were the Pointer, Irish Water Spaniel, Clumber Spaniel, Cocker Spaniel, Sussex Spaniel, Chesapeake Bay Retriever, and Gordon, Irish, and English Setters.[1] With the exception of the Chesey, the ancestors of these dogs were the foundation of the English Setter. Primarily responsible for the modern English Setter were two English sportsmen, Edward Laverack, Esq. (1797-1877) and R. LL. Purcell Llewellin, Esq. (1840-1925). Along with such notable English colleagues as the Rev. A. Harrison (breeder of Ponto and Old Moll) and Mr. Statter and Sir Vincent Corbet (breeders of Duke and Rhoebe), they founded the breed, as we know it.[2]

Edward Laverack purchased Ponto and Old Moll from the Rev. Harrison around 1825 and with them began a breeding program that

1

continued for fifty years. In 1872 he published a book titled *The Setter.* Reprinted in 1945, this book, subtitled *Notices of the most eminent Breeds now extant; Instructions on how to breed, rear, and break; Dog shows; Field trials; General Management; Etc.,* was one of the first specialty breeders/dog show books ever. Laverack details his breeding program and chronicles his development of the modern "bench" or show English Setter. Laverack dedicated his book to his friend and admirer R. LL. Purcell Llewellin, Esq.

Llewellin was a dog show competitor, an avid hunter, and a field trial competitor. He purchased a number of Setters from Laverack and attempted his own breedings and outcrosses. One of his Setters, a bitch named "Flame," figured in the beginnings of the great Mallwyd Kennels. Finding that Laverack's Setters were not competitive with the Pointers and Spaniels he encountered at field trials, Llewellin obtained two male Setters, Dan and Dick, from Mr. Statter. These dogs were from the Duke-Rhoebe strain created by Statter and Corbet. By breeding Dan and Dick to his Laverack bitches he created a smaller, less-coated bird dog that was the beginning of the modern field strain of English Setter.[3]

Thus it is that English Setters, unlike any other Sporting Breed, have two officially registered and distinct types—a bench or show type and a field type. Since English Setter fanciers commonly refer to the bench or show type as Laveracks and the field type as Llewellins, these terms will be used in this book.[4]

The Early Years

The modern English Setter show dog was developed from Laverack and Llewellin stock in England and Scotland by several sportsman breeders. Among the most influential were these:

- Mr. Thomas Steadman—Mallwyd Kennels
- Mr. D. K. Steadman (Thomas' brother) —Maesydd Kennels
- Dr. L. Thurston Price—Crombie Kennels [5]

Thomas Steadman used get from Llewellin's bitches Flame and Carrie (these were the Laverack/Irish (Red and White) Setter outcrosses that Llewellin bred) as the foundation of the great Mallwyd Kennels. In 1916 Mallwyd produced a prepotent sire named *Ch. Mallwyd Albert*, who was the foundation sire of the Selkirk, Grayland, Southboro, Rowland, Crombie, Rummey, Shiplake, Stylish, and Maesydd kennels.[6] By the late 1800s and early 1900s, Mallwyd English Setter stock would made its way into the United States and Canada, where along with Crombie dogs it had a major influence on the modern English Setter show dog in America.

English Setter show activity in the United States actually began on the West Coast, because from Vancouver, British Columbia, to Van Nuys, California, English Setter breeders were importing stock from England and Scotland and creating the modern show English Setter. As early as 1900 T. P. McConnell and his son N. (Norm) P. McConnell began importing Mallwyd Setters into Canada and established their famous Selkirk Kennels in Vancouver, B.C. In a stud dog advertisement in an early dog publication (circa 1904), T.P. McConnell discussed Mallwyd Bob, an early winner and famous English Champion found in the pedigree of Rackets Rummey.[7]

Ch. Mallwyd Bob circa 1904

(photo from the author's collection)

His son, Norm McConnell, was responsible for breeding a litter that contained two of the great foundation bitches in breed history—*Selkirk Snooksie* and her litter sister *Selkirk Mallhawk Juliet.* In an article titled "Mallhawk Jeff" in the September 1948 issue of *Popular Dogs*, Earl Kruger (owner of Selkirk Mallhawk Juliet) says,

> *Snooksie? Without her there never would have been a Rummey Stagboro, Sturdy Max, Maro and the whole line of fine Setters that came from these dogs. And Juliet? From her, Mallhawk Jeff, Rip, Lola, Enid, Alice, Lem and now Mary of Blue Bar* [Ch. Mary of Blue Bar was Group 3 at the 1949 Morris & Essex KC]….
>
> *Yes, these two bitches have their place in this world.*

Another Vancouver, B.C., kennel, Willgress Setters, founded by W. T. Willgress, also used Mallwyd stock as its foundation. This kennel produced **Ch. Sir Orkney of Willgress Jr.,** acquired by J. J. Sinclair of Orkney Kennels in San Francisco. Another noteworthy Willgress Setter was Sinclair's **Ch. Rowlands Lady Bird**, which went back-to-back Best in Show at the Oakland and Del Monte, California, kennel clubs before she was unfortunately lost to pneumonia.[8]

Founded by A. J. Kruger, Mallhawk Kennels began in Oregon and was later moved to Van Nuys, California, by his son Earl Kruger. Mallhawk was founded on Mallwyd and Mohawk stock (hence the name Mallhawk from *Mall*wyd and Mo*hawk).* Mallhawk setters are found in many of the famous English Setter kennels, most notably C. N. Myers' Blue Bar Kennels. In 1935 Myers purchased *Ch. Mallhawk's Jeff,* the dog that became the foundation sire for his famous Blue Bar Kennels. Dr. Carl Sillman (whose research on C. N. Myers' Blue Bar Kennels was invaluable for this book) said that C. N. badgered Ray Hurley for months to sell him Jeff; C. N. knew a good Setter when he saw one!

As Earl Kruger wrote in his September 1948 *Popular Dogs* article,

> *The litter comes and there he is, what a pup—Mallhawk Jeff! He is great right from birth. When he comes along, we ship him East and Ray Hurley gets him. He grows*

that good New York coat, and the following year Ray brings him out. We want to start where the going is really tough, where it takes a real champion to win a blue. How does he go? Three five pointers in a row!! New York, Baltimore, and Morris and Essex. And at the Bronx, New York, Dr. Buck puts him all the way to Best in Show. Jeff is acclaimed as the greatest living English setter.

In 1905 J. J. Sinclair immigrated to San Francisco, California, from his native Scotland and founded the Orkney Kennels using stock from Mallwyd and Maesydd. A compatriot of Dr. L. Thurston Price of Crombie fame, like a number of Scottish breeders he had a profound influence on English Setters. His dogs were very successful at early West Coast dog shows, with *Ch. Sir Orkney of Willgress Jr.* winning multiple Best in Shows. This dog sired *Ch. Modern Maid of Stucile* (originally Modern Maid of Orkney), which was ultimately acquired by C. N. Myers and became one of Blue Bar's foundation bitches.[9] James Haring remarked in his 1948 *Popular Dogs* article that "most critics have felt that Modern Maid was one of the finest ES bitches ever bred."

On the East Coast, Henry F. Steigerwald's Stagboro Kennels in Auburn, NY, crossed Mallwyd setters from Norm McConnell's Selkirk Kennels (especially Selkirk's Snooksie) with Laverack setters from Sweden (through Int. Ch. Spiron and Spiron Jagersbo, owned by Eric Bergishagen Sr.) to produce the great *Rummey Stagboro* in 1929. In his book, Davis Tuck declared that Rummey Stagboro was the prepotent sire of the first several decades of English Setter greats inasmuch as he was the foremost of the Mallwyd strain that so heavily influenced the modern English Setter show dog.[10]

Eric Bergishagen Sr. emigrated from Denmark in 1921 and founded Jagersbo Kennels in Michigan. He imported a number of English Setters from Scandinavia, England, and Germany as well as breeding a number of important dogs in the early 1930s.[11]

The years between 1916 (when Ch. Mallwyd Albert was whelped) and 1930 can be considered the "early years" of English Setter show dogs in the United States. For one thing, the breed was still in the

Rummey Stagboro
            (photo from archives of Bill and Lovey Trotter- Flecka's)

process of becoming established in America and Canada; for another, before 1924 dog shows were not conducted as they are today, and few show records were kept. But some English Setters stood out. Among them were the following:

- Ch. Manzanita (whelped in 1909), owned by J. J. Sinclair, Orkney Kennels

- Int. Ch. McConnell's Nori (whelped 08/1924), owned by N. P. McConnell, Selkirk Kennels

- Int. Ch. Spiron (whelped 04/1916) and Int. Ch. Rackets Rummey (whelped 12/1922), owned by Eric Bergishagen Sr., Jagersbo Kennels

- Ch. Mallhawks Rackets Boy (whelped 03/1926), owned by A. J. Kruger, Mallhawk Kennels

- Rummey Stagboro (whelped 08/1929), owned by Henry F. Steigerwald, Stagboro Kennels

These were not only top show dogs in their day, but had a significant impact on the breed as well.[12] Ch. Manzanita was the foundation sire of Orkney Kennels. Int. Ch. McConnell's Nori was the sire of two important bitches, Selkirk's Snooksie and her litter sister Selkirk's Juliet. Selkirk's Snooksie was the dam of the great Rummey Stagboro.[13] Bred by Henry Steigerwald, with a pedigree including Int. Chs. Spiron and Rackets Rummey, this dog is credited by Davis Tuck in his encyclopedic *The Complete English Setter* as the foundation of the "winning strain" of English Setter show dogs. The descendants of Rummey Stagboro number among the premier English show dogs right up to the present day.

Dr. A. A. Mitten's Happy Valley Kennels in Philadelphia also began to influence English Setter show dogs with Crombie imports; this was the home of the great Ch. Pilot of Crombie of Happy Valley.[14]

Ch. Fred of Crombie (a grandson of Am./Eng. Ch. Mallwyd Albert) won an amazing 5 AKC Best in Shows in 1929, while Ch. Pilot of Crombie of Happy Valley was poised to make his mark in the show ring in the 1930s.

Puppy judging 1928 Morris & Essex K.C.
(photo courtesy of St. Hubert's Animal Welfare Center, Madison N.J.)

Thus we have set the stage for the next decade. English Setters in America have been developed from Mallwyd and Crombie stock with Swedish elements (from Eric Bergishagen's Jagersbo kennels). In Rummey Stagboro, a dominant sire has appeared, and several major kennels are active. Still, only about three hundred dog shows were held annually in the entire country—about five or six each weekend. With so few contests, the best dogs in every breed and group would constantly meet and vie for top honors, and for a dog of any breed to become a "big winner" meant beating the top competition week in and week out. How did English Setters do? Exceedingly well....Read on.

Endnotes

1. AKC web site, http://www.akc.org

2. Davis Tuck, *The Complete English Setter*, 1951.

3. Ibid.

4. In her book *The Essence of Setters* (2002), Marsha Hall Brown calls these "false labels" and gives detailed rationale. Also see *All Setters* by Lloyd Freeman (1931) for his detailed examination of Laverack and Llewellin breedings.

5. Tuck, *The Complete English Setter*.

6. Ibid.

7. Stud dog advertisement, circa 1904.

8. Margaret Hawn, English Setter column, *Popular Dogs*, November 1969.

9. Ibid.

10. Tuck, *The Complete English Setter*.

11. Interview with Eric Bergishagen Jr., *The Sporting Life*, November/December 1992.

12. James S. Haring Jr., "Back to Mallwyd," *Popular Dogs*, September 1948.

13. Earl C. Kruger, "Mallhawk Jeff," *Popular Dogs,* September 1948.

14. *AKC Gazettes,* 1928-30.

*Best of Breed judging at 1933 Morris & Essex K.C., (from left to right)
Ch. Hearthstone's Orkney Chief, Maesydd Modesty of Bromiley (Best of
Winners handled by Harry Hill) and Ch. Gilroy's Chief Topic (Best of Breed
handled by W.F. Gilroy) the judge is Thomas D. Buck.*
(photo courtesy of St. Hubert's Animal Welfare Center, Madison N.J.)

Chapter Two

The Golden Era, 1930-60: The 1930s

The Rise of the English

The first thirty years of the twentieth century had witnessed the introduction of the Laverack type of bench setter into the United States and Canada from England, Sweden, and Germany, as well as the beginnings of breeding programs in newly established English Setter kennels. By 1930 these programs had borne fruit, and the English Setter was poised to make its mark. And what a mark it was. The 1930s saw the beginning of the golden Era of English Setter show dogs in America. In the AKC show history of English Setters, 41 have won 5 or more All-Breed AKC Best in Shows. (Literally hundreds of English Setters have won a single to 4 All-Breed Best in Shows, but this book deals with the "best of the best.") Surprisingly, 12 of these 41, nearly *one-third* of all great English, won their red, white, and blue ribbons in the 1930s. At a time of relatively few AKC shows (compared to today) these majestic animals were among the top show breeds. The first of these top dogs was *Ch. Fred of Crombie*, one of the fine dogs bred by Dr. L. Thurston Price of the famous Crombie Kennels in Scotland. D. C. Kok, a member of the first Board of Directors of

ESA, imported him into the United States in 1928. Fred won *5 BIS in 1929* before retiring from the ring.[1]

One criterion for inclusion in this book is a Group or Best in Show win at the old Morris & Essex Kennel Club. It is difficult today to comprehend the significance or importance of the Morris & Essex. This show was held on the polo fields of the Giralda Farms Estate of Mrs. Geraldine Rockefeller Dodge. Mrs. Dodge (daughter of William Rockefeller) hosted this show from 1927 to 1957 (with interruptions for the WWII years), and it was instantly the event of the year. Elaborate tenting was erected; Mrs. Dodge donated sterling silver trophies that were presented to virtually every class winner. The photos of the trophy table at Morris & Essex are simply stunning. Box lunches were provided to exhibitors and spectators, and news camera towers were erected. The entry quickly rose to more than four thousand dogs—this at a time when most shows drew fewer than one thousand entries. All of the greatest show dogs went to Morris & Essex.[2] There is no comparison to this show today. It combined the prestige of Westminster with the scale of Crufts, all wrapped in a beautiful venue hosted by a legendary dog enthusiast. Mrs. Dodge imported breeding stock, raised dogs (including English Setters[3]), and later became a renowned AKC judge. She judged the 1960

Ch. Inglehurst Reward winning the Group at the 1930 Morris & Essex K.C. (photo courtesy of St. Hubert's Animal Welfare Center, Madison N.J.)

ESAA National Specialty (which was the first year it was held in conjunction with the newly formed Combined Setter Clubs of America). *Ch. Inglehurst Reward*, owned by former AKC President Charles T. Inglee, won the *Group at the Morris and Essex* KC show in 1930.[4]

With the growing popularity of AKC bench shows, the *English Setter Association of America (ESAA)* was formed in 1931 to promote the breeding and exhibition of bench show Setters. The existing English Setter *Club* of America was focused on Field Trials. ESAA held its first National Specialty show in 1932 and has held one every year thereafter. This book will recognize the winners of Best in Specialty Show (BISS) at this most prestigious of all English Setter Breed-level competitions.

The first English Setter of the 1930s to rise to national prominence was Dr. A. A. Mitten's great *Ch. Blue Dan of Happy Valley*. Davis Tuck described this magnificent Setter as a compact, well-balanced, open-marked blue Belton about 24 inches at the withers and about 60 pounds (according to the pedigree published in Davis Tuck's *Complete English Setter*). Studying his photo, we can see his balance, angulation, and beautiful head. Ch. Blue Dan of Happy Valley won *24 AKC BIS* between 1930 and 1933.[5] This ranks as the fifth best of all time among English Setters. In addition to his All-Breed BIS, Blue Dan won *Best American-Bred in Show* at the *Westminster Kennel Club in 1931 and 1933*. (This award, made if the overall BIS winner at Westminster was not bred in America, was discontinued in 1961.) Blue Dan won the *Sporting Group at Westminster in 1931 and 1933*. He was second in the Group in 1932 and took consecutive Group 2s at Morris & Essex in 1931 and 1932.

Blue Dan's 1931 appearance at the Garden and the Best in Show judging was widely reported and is one of the legendary Westminster stories. In an April 1970 article in *Popular Dogs* titled "Memories of Westminster" by Arthur Fredrick Jones, the "Dean of the Dog Writers," wrote the following:

> *In 1931…Tyler Morse did Best in Show. In that final she* [the Wire Fox Terrier Ch. Pendley Calling of Blarney, who was BIS in 1930] *met, among others, the*

English Setter, Ch. Blue Dan of Happy Valley, owned by Dr. Arthur A. Mitten, the medical doctor, who for years was head of all Philadelphia's transit, surface, and elevated transportation lines and even taxicabs.... Well, as it happened, the galleries fell in love with Blue Dan's way of coming and going and when the judge gave the Best in Show to the Wire, the wave of booing was comparable only to some of today's hippy demonstrations.

Ch. Blue Dan of Happy Valley
  (photo from album of Bill and Lovey Trotter- Flecka's)

In his 1980 book *My Times with Dogs,* Walter Fletcher, the longtime writer for *The New York Times,* relates that same incident.

The 1931 show is one I'll never forget....In 1931 the cheers were for a flashy blue ticked English Setter, Dr. A.A. Mitten's Ch. Blue Dan of Happy Valley. When [BIS judge] Tyler Morse pointed to Pendley Calling [the Wire Fox Terrier], there was prolonged booing.

What an absolutely magnificent exhibition Blue Dan must have put on! Not only is it widely known that the gallery at Westminster is one of the most knowledgeable at any dog show, but until I read accounts of the 1931 show, I had never heard of any gallery booing. And this was 1931, when the public was considerably more courteous than today. Blue Dan was also (fittingly) the winner of the first-ever *ESAA National Specialty in 1932*. So as the 1930s began, English Setters were among the top AKC show dogs.

Another of Dr. A. A. Mitten's Happy Valley dogs, *Ch. The Country Gentleman*, followed Blue Dan. The Country Gentleman won *14 AKC BIS* (eighth best all-time record) in his career between 1932 and 1936 as well as the second *ESAA National Specialty in 1933.*[6] Bred in Los Angeles out of imported Crombie and J. J. Sinclair's Orkney stock, he was acquired by Happy Valley Kennels and shipped east in 1932.

In 1931 Dr. Thurston Price sent another of his dogs, *Ch. Pilot of Crombie of Happy Valley*, to live at Dr. Mitten's Happy Valley Kennels. This open-marked blue Belton with a solid blue ear was more modern looking than his predecessors at 25 ½ inches and an athletic 60 pounds. Pilot won *7 BIS* between 1934 and 1937 as well as the *1934 and 1936 ESAA Nationals*, and was the first English Setter to win multiple Nationals.[7]

Ch. Pilot of Crombie of Happy Valley
(photo from archives of Bill and Lovey Trotter- Flecka's)

In the January 1935 *AKC Gazette*, A. L. Jones of Marional Farms Kennels described the 1934 Philadelphia KC, which was also the site of the 1934 ESAA Nationals. The famous photo of the Happy Valley bench, taken at this show, appears in C. Bede Maxwell's *The Truth about Sporting Dogs*, and what follows is an excerpt from that 1935 column:

> [in the benching photo] *There were puppies and young-sters attending their first show, barking and getting tangled up in their bench chains. There were matured dogs used to the excitement of the show game, but sitting alert and eager to slip into a show leash, and there were the seasoned campaigners, bored with the excitement of the youngsters and the admiration of the public, stretched out asleep, utterly oblivious of the fact that they were part of this marvelous picture. Even old Blue Dan* [Ch. Blue Dan of Happy Valley] *was there, looking as handsome as ever, and on his feet most of the two days, barking his joy at being back in harness again.*
>
> *Among this array of Champions, near champions, young-sters, and puppies, was one who maintained a quiet, dignified air, as if by some unknown dog sense he was already aware of the honors which were in store for him. Pilot of Crombie* [of Happy Valley], *one of the greatest of the Crombies ever imported to this country was at this show to come into his own by defeating for best of breed not only his kennel mate champions, but in addition that sterling performer of the year, Ch. Gilroy's Chief Topic.... In the Sporting Group, he faced some keen competition, and went to the top in this group under the expert eye of Mr. Smalley, and to cap a wonderful performance, he carried off Best in Show from some of the most famous group winners in the game, and I do not believe Dr. Jarrett ever had the pleasure of making a more popular Best in Show award. Here was performance par excel-lence in a dog that combines the two prime requisites of*

an English Setter, a true symmetrical movement that has
power plus, and size with uniformity of structure that
denotes beauty and utility.

What an amazing weekend! Pilot won the ESAA National Specialty in the morning and went Best in Show that evening. It doesn't get much better.

Breaking the string of three straight ESAA National wins by Happy Valley Kennels was *Ch. Robin Hood of Marional*, who won the *1935 ESAA National Specialty* along with *9 AKC Best in Shows* between 1935 and 1937.[8] Mr. and Mrs. A. L. Jones of Marional Farms Kennels—the same Mr. A.L. Jones who wrote the column quoted above—owned him.

Ch. Robin Hood of Marional

(from 1938 AKC Blue Book of Dogs)

Another of the foremost English Setters of the 1930s was *Ch. Gilroy's Chief Topic*. Bred, owned, and shown by William F. Gilroy and later acquired by Mrs. Allan Ryan, co-owner of Prune's Own Kennels. Topic had a long show career (1932 through 1939), as is typical of English Setters. His best years were between the ages of three and nine, when he won *13 AKC BIS*.[9] This very light blue Belton was in the mold of Blue Dan at about 24 inches and 60 pounds. Looking at his photograph (and ignoring the 1930s-style grooming) we see another well-balanced Setter with a fine front and pleasing head. A head photograph of Chief Topic in the *1964 ESAA Annual* (a "yearbook" of the association) shows the clean chiseled lines, rounded skull, and low ear set that have all the ingredients of the modern English Setter head. The photograph at the beginning of this chapter shows Chief Topic winning Best of Breed at the 1933 Morris & Essex KC with Mr. Gilroy handling.

Ch. Gilroy's Chief Topic
(photo from archives of Gus Polley – Skidby)

The primary rival of Chief Topic and Pilot was the great *Ch. Sturdy Max*, bred by the Sturdy Dog Food Company and ultimately owned by Maridor Kennels. This magnificent orange Belton is truly the prototype of the current English Setter. Whelped in 1932, sired by Rummey Stagboro (he also included Selkirk, Grayland, and Rowland bloodlines in his pedigree), Max stood 25 ¾ inches tall and gracefully bore a powerful 65 pounds.[10] His show record was an impressive *13 BIS* between 1934 and 1937.[11] In *1937* Sturdy Max had one of the most momentous weekends of any English Setter. That year, when the ESAA National Specialty was held in conjunction with the prestigious *Morris & Essex KC*, Sturdy Max won the *ESAA National Specialty* in the morning and *Best in Show* in the evening. In the *1969 ESAA Annual*, Gordon Parham, a renowned

English Setter breeder (Parpoint Kennels), handler (he was kennel manager for the famous Maridor Kennels), and AKC judge was asked to recall English Setters "I would like to have owned." While he mentioned many famous dogs, he said this about Ch. Sturdy Max,

> *During the evening before the 1937 Morris and Essex Show...several handlers and exhibitors watched a one dog show. Charlie Palmer* [a famous handler of the 1930s and '40s] *posed this dog for the gallery, which included Col. R. L. Dick Davis, Charlie Davis* [handler for C. N. Myers' Blue Bar Kennels], *Frank Feldschmidt, Ward Snaar, Davis Tuck, Dr. Fletcher Vinson* [Rockboro Kennels], *Phil Marsh and me...the dog was Ch. Sturdy Max....I predicted that Max would go BIS the next day. Over an entry of 4104, of which 123 were English Setters, he won....Dr. Samuel Milbank pointed at him while 60,000 spectators cheered and newsreel cameras click from atop specially erected towers for the occasion....If I were to have only one* [English Setter] *it would have to have been Ch. Sturdy Max....I'll continue thinking of him as the nearly "perfect piece to see."*

Ch. Sturdy Max & Charles Palmer Group 1 photo 1937 Morris & Essex K.C. (photo courtesy of St. Hubert's Animal Welfare Center, Madison N.J.)

Mrs. C. Bede Maxwell, the great Australian author (*The Truth About Sporting Dogs*), AKC judge, and German Shorthair breeder, said this about Sturdy Max: "Every aspirant judge should be expected to memorize the type structure, stance, and presentation of this great dog, to be engraved in such depth as to be able to carry it through the span of a judging lifetime."[12]

Surely if he carried the modern style of coat, he would be competitive today. A son of Rummey Stagboro, Max in turn sired the great Maridor Kennels "brothers" Daro and Maro (more about them later), and the great Delwed "brothers" Sir Guy and Cedric, and thus continued the "winning strain."

Ch. Sturdy Max
(photo from archives of Bill and Lovey Trotter-Flecka's)

Throughout the 1930s, many other English Setters were making their marks in the eastern and central parts of the nation, and in California, J. J. Sinclair continued to have success with his Orkney setters. ***Ch. Sir Orkney of Willgress Jr.***, son of his famous stud, Ch. Orkney Willgress, won *5 AKC BIS* between 1934 and 1937.[13]

As the 1930s drew to a close, ***Ch. Modern Boy of Stucile*** (another Rummey Stagboro son and one of C. N. Myers' first specials) made his presence known in the show ring by winning *8 AKC BIS* in just two short show seasons (1938-39).[14] In 1938 ***Ch. Daro of Maridor*** became the only English Setter to take the overall ***Best in Show title at the Westminster Kennel Club***, when he won "the Garden" at only eleven months old (beating the great Ch. Pilot of Crombie of Happy Valley for the breed win)! Proving that this win was only the beginning, he went on to win 4 more BIS and 2 ESAA Nationals in his career. Like his sire, Ch. Sturdy Max, he and his litter brother Ch. Maro of Maridor were to become English Setters of historic significance.

Ch. Daro of Maridor
(photo from archives of Bill and Lovey Trotter- Flecka's)

The ***1938 ESAA National*** was won by ***Ch. Lakelands Yuba***, an open-marked blue Belton of 25½ inches and about 64 pounds owned by Charles Palmer and later acquired by Maridor Kennels. Another of the "winning strain" sired by Rummey Stagboro, Yuba had that wonderful topline and tail set that we like in our show English. Well-laid-back shoulders and a deep chest accentuated his powerful movement in the ring. The photos suggest a slightly larger headpiece that we see today. As with many great English Setters, Yuba began his career going Winners Dog at the 1936 ESAA Nationals, and two years later he won the National.

The decade closed in ***1939*** with another of Clinton N. Myers' Blue Bar Kennels dogs making its mark as ***Ch. Deli of Blue Bar*** won

Ch. Lakelands Yuba

(photo from The AKC Blue Book 1938)

BISS at the ESAA National. Deli, a daughter of the great Pilot of Crombie of Happy Valley, was the *first English Setter Bitch to win a National.* Furthermore, her win marked the first time the *daughter* of an English Setter National BISS winner had also won the National BISS.

Ch. Deli of Blue Bar

(photo courtesy of Dr. Carl Sillman, ESAA Historian)

The English Setter kennels of Happy Valley, Blue Bar, Maridor, Jagersbo, Mallhawk, Orkney, and Stagboro, along with the Crombie imports, produced a quality of stock that served as the foundation of our modern bloodlines. From Rummey Stagboro through Sturdy Max, into the Maridor and Delwed brothers and the Blue Bar dogs, the "winning strain" (as Davis Tuck pointed out) can be traced to these great show dogs. This remarkable decade saw *nine English Setters* winning a combined total of *98 AKC Best in Show* awards between *1929 and 1939*. These were not the only English Setters who won Best in Shows, just the ones who did it over and over again. English Setters won or placed in the Sporting Group at Westminster seven of ten years and at Morris & Essex six of ten years. They won a Best in Show at each of these shows as well.

Given these accomplishments, the breed could well expect to retain its standing as a top all-breed show dog. The next decades would prove this very true indeed.

1938 ESA Futurity
  (photo courtesy of St. Hubert's Animal Welfare Center, Madison N.J.)

Endnotes

1. Richard Fox, pedigree research, *AKC Gazettes,* 1929-30.

2. Dr. A. Duane Butherus, re-creation of Morris & Essex, *Dogs in Review,* February 2000.

3. In 1930 Mrs. Dodge purchased from the Crombie Kennels in Scotland, "the finest draft of setters and pointers that has ever been secured by an individual fancier" *(Popular Dogs,* February 1931). The article goes on to describe Ch. Marvel of Crombie, which was one of the dogs in this purchase:

   Marvel of Crombie is the most outstanding English setter in Britain and his show record is a wonderful one. He has been shown at the following: Scottish Kennel Club show, 1929; National show Birmingham, 1929; Crufts, 1930; Cardiff, 1930; Darlington, 1930; Edinburgh, 1930 and the Crystal Palace [KC], 1930, winning first and championship at each. All these shows are noted for the strength of competition in this breed. At the National show in Birmingham (with which is held the Setter and Pointer Club show) Marvel was awarded the cup for the best setter (any variety) or pointer....Marvel is summed up by one of the oldest authorities on the setter breed as the best he has ever seen. Mrs. Dodge gets what is admitted to be the best English setter of all-time....Mrs. Dodge's English setters arrived in New York during the month of November, 1930.

4. Morris & Essex Kennel Club archives.

5. *AKC Gazettes,* 1930-40.

6. Ibid.

7. Ibid.

8. Ibid.

9. Ibid.

10. Davis Tuck, *The Complete English Setter,* 1951.

11. AKC *Gazettes,* 1930-40.

12. C. Bede Maxwell, "Setters...the Mishandling of," *Popular Dogs.*

13. AKC *Gazettes,* 1930-40.

14. Ibid.

Chapter Three

The Golden Era, 1930-60: The 1940s

The Decade of the Brothers

As the 1930s drew to a close, English Setters had become a breed to be reckoned with at dog shows. Combining the athleticism of the sporting dog with the beauty and grace of a long-coated Setter, English Setters made a perfect combination for the sportsman/fancier of the day. The seminal kennels of Clover Ridge (Gilroy), Happy Valley, Jagersbo, Lakeland, Mallhawk, Orkney, Stagboro, and Selkirk were about to be joined by kennels founded on their stock. Most notable among these were the Blue Bar, Delwed, Maridor, Rock Falls, and Silvermine Kennels.

As mentioned in the last chapter, two litter brothers, sired by Ch. Sturdy Max, had come on the scene in 1938. After going *BIS* at *Westminster in 1938*, *Ch. Daro of Maridor* went on to win *back-to-back ESAA National Specialties in 1940 and 1941*, the first English Setter to win two Nationals in succession. Between 1938 and 1943, Ch. Daro of Maridor won *5 AKC Best in Shows* for his owner, Charles G. Diamon of Connecticut.[1] Daro was an open-marked orange Belton just over 25 inches and about 65 pounds. Looking at his photo (and remembering that the "style of the stack" for many years was "head out and tail down"), one can visualize how this dog looked when holding his head proud and tail level. His wonderful neck blends into

Ch. Maro of Maridor
Photo courtesy of Dr. Carl Sillman, ESAA Historian

his shoulders, his tail is "an extension of his back," and his angulation predicts that he can move.

But as good as he was, there was one arguably better—his brother. *Ch. Maro of Maridor*, owned by Mrs. Wilfred Kennedy of Detroit, Michigan, was shown at exactly the same time as his brother, and in his show career between 1938 and 1943 Maro won an incredible *55 AKC Best in Show*—at that time the AKC record for any breed![2] Maro was whelped on March 18, 1937, and was winning Best in Shows before he was two years old. *Maro had 10 BIS before he was three* and won the *Group at Morris & Essex in 1938* just a month after his brother won BIS at Westminster, and both dogs did this from the classes! Maro again won the *Group at Morris & Essex in 1940*. He was the *top AKC dog* (in terms of number of BIS) from *1940* until his retirement at the age of six in *1943*. One of the many memorable moments in his career occurred at the 1943 Cincinnati KC show. In an article titled "A Century of Dogs" in the February 2000 issue of *Dogs in Review*, Bo Bengston recounts the following:

> *A fight erupts during Best in Show judging at Cin-*
> *cinnati, when the famous English Setter, Ch. Maro of*

*Maridor is attacked by the Group winning Great Dane.
"Maro was anxious to lick anything in sight, and there
was no denying his domination in the ring."[3] He puts on
"one of the finest exhibitions of his career" and wins his
46th BIS.*

Maro was an open-marked orange Belton with beautiful flecking
and white fringe. Standing 25 inches at the withers, he was shown at
a trim 60 pounds. Maro's photo shows a well-balanced dog with a
graceful neck blending into well-laid-back shoulders. The head is
held proudly, and one can readily surmise that he held it that way in
the ring. Ch. Maro of Maridor still holds the second-best record for
AKC Best in Shows in the history of English Setters.

*Ch. Maro of Maridor in Group 1938
(photo courtesy of St. Hubert's Animal Welfare Center, Madison N.J.)*

The Maridors were not the only English Setter brothers winning
Best in Shows in the early 1940s. George F. Wedel's Delwed Kennels
in central Michigan also bred to Ch. Sturdy Max and produced
another remarkable pair of brothers. The first, *Ch. Sir Guy of Delwed,*
owned by F. J. Feldschmidt of Illinois, was shown largely in the Midwest between 1940 and 1945. In those years, he won a remarkable *23
AKC BIS*, then the third-best record for an English Setter (behind
only Maro of Maridor and Blue Dan of Happy Valley).[4]

Ch. Sir Guy of Delwed
(photo from archives of Gus Polley – Skidby)

Ch. Cedric of Delwed
(photo from archives of Bill and Lovey Trotter- Flecka's)

Sir Guy's litter brother ***Ch. Cedric of Delwed***, owned and shown by George Wedel largely in the Ohio River Valley states, had *7 BIS* between 1939 and 1944.[5] He was a very evenly marked orange Belton with a light lemon eye patch on his non-show side (seen in his picture). His head shows the nice muzzle length and stop of a classic English Setter, with a long neck flowing into well-laid-back shoulders. His low ear set compliments his front perfectly. He has a moderate length of back with just the right tail set, and is beginning to show the longer coat desired of the bench show setters.

The reader should pause and think about this for a moment. The English Setter fancy was witness to two pairs of brothers, shown in the same six-year period, and winning a combined:

- *Ninety AKC Best in Shows*
- *Two ESAA National Specialties*
- *BIS at Westminster Kennel Club*

Yet more amazing is that all four were sired by the great Ch. Sturdy Max! Here is further support for Davis Tuck's conception of a "winning strain." And, despite the dominance in the 1930s of the blue Belton, all four were orange Beltons.

Although Setters from the large kennels of Delwed, Blue Bar, and Maridor were dominant, smaller hobby kennels founded on "winning strain" stock achieved noteworthy successes in the show ring. A Colorado dog bred and owned by Mr. C. F. Cusak, Rancho Ridge Kennels, *Ch. Dive Bomber* (a Sturdy Max grandson), won *5 BIS* between 1943 and 1945.[6] Unfortunately, he died suddenly while in Texas on a dog show circuit.[7] On the *ESAA National Specialty* scene, *Ch. Big Boy of Rockboro* (a Rummey Stagboro grandson), owned by Dr. Fletcher L. Vinson (president of ESAA 1941-45 and 1948-50), won the 1942 National.

In New York, Prune's Own Kennels, owned by Mrs. George B. St. George, the first woman president of ESAA (1946-47) and her daughter, Mrs. Allen (Priscilla) Ryan,[8] acquired famous English Setter show dogs such as Ch. Gilroy's Chief Topic and Ch. Maro of Maridor and used Rummey Stagboro and Sturdy Max offspring to develop several winning Setters. Their *Ch. Prune's Own Maxson's Dawn* took *BISS at the ESAA National Specialty in 1944*. Another of their dogs, *Ch. Prune's Own Palmer*, owned by N. Burfoot of Elizabeth City, North Carolina, and handled by Arthur Mulvihill Jr., won the *1946 ESAA National* and went *Group 1 at Westminster KC* that same year. He finished his show career with an admirable *3 AKC BIS*.[9]

Other notable show dogs from the early 1940s include ***Ch. Blue Bar Limited***, who won 5 AKC Best in Shows in 1940, and ***Ch. Lem of Blue Bar***, who in *1943* gave C. N. Myers' kennel his second *ESAA Nationals* victory.[10] Lem of Blue Bar was the dog chosen to illustrate the description of the English Setter Standard in the famous September 1948 issue of *Popular Dogs* and *all four* editions of Davis Tuck's book, to say nothing of being the illustration of the Standard *before* and *after* it was twice revised by ESAA! No finer compliment can be paid to an English Setter than to be chosen by Davis Tuck and Elsworth Howell as the Standard of the breed. Ch. Lem of Blue Bar is also the *only dog ever used* in the Official English Setter Association of America membership guide to illustrate the Standard.

Ch. Blue Bar Limited (photo courtesy of Dr. Carl Sillman, ESAA Historian)

Ch. Lem of Blue Bar (photo from archives of Gus Polley – Skidby)

C. N. Myers' Blue Bar dogs continued to win during the second half of the 1940s. Probably the greatest of the Blue Bar dogs, *Ch. Rip of Blue Bar* won *7 AKC Best in Shows* between 1946 and 1948 as well as *two ESAA National Specialties*, the first in *1945* (from the classes) and the second in *1947*.[11] He was awarded the *1947 Quaker Oats Trophy* for the dog (all breeds) winning the most Group 1s in the Eastern Region. Rip was a big, richly colored orange Belton, standing 26 inches and shown at 68 pounds. His photo shows a powerful dog with a tremendous front end. Laid-back shoulders with excellent angulation and a level topline to well-angled rear quarters must have given this dog stunning side gait as he went around the ring. Sad to say, Rip died in an accident en route to a dog show in 1948.[12]

Ch. Rip of Blue Bar in Group
(photo from archives of Gus Polley – Skidby)

Davis Tuck's Silvermine Kennels were well represented during this time with his great *Ch. Silvermine Wagabond* winning *back-to-back ESAA Nationals in 1948 and 1949*. Upholding the honor of the great Blue Beltons of the '30s, this descendent of Rummey Stagboro and Sturdy Max was a stunningly handsome male at 26 inches and 70 pounds. Handled his entire career by his owner Virginia Tuck, he stands as the epitome of the classic English Setter. Marsha Hall Brown, daughter of Commander Thomas Hall of Stone Gables Kennels, was quoted in a 1982 interview in *The Setter Quarterly* as saying,

> *He* [Ch. Silvermine Wagabond] *was a sparkling blue belton with lots of white, and beautiful clear markings. Beautifully put down as only Virginia Tuck could have put down a dog. He was a handsome, classic Englishman, and he was the first one I remember very clearly as being a gorgeous dog.*

In my dog-eared copy of Davis Tuck's *The Complete English Setter* is a note my wife made when we first became active in the breed in the early '70s. It reads, "Love this one!! Neck & topline." As she observed, his head and neck are smoothly sculptured and blend into a beautiful topline. The current AKC Standard for English Setters calls for a topline that "in motion or standing appears level or sloping slightly without sway or drop from the withers to tail forming a graceful outline of medium length." Study his photo as you read those words. With Wagabond and Lem of Blue Bar, a better visual representation would be hard to find.

Ch. Silvermine Wagabond

(photo courtesy Virginia Tuck Hall)

On the basis of AKC Best in Shows and ESAA National Specialty BISS, the 1940s were dominated by dogs from five famous kennels: Maridor, Delwed, Blue Bar, Prune's Own, and Silvermine. *These dogs won 105 BIS ribbons and nine of ten ESAA Nationals.*

At the major shows, Westminster and Morris & Essex, these dogs plus *Ch. End O'Maine Sorry* (from Hollis Wilson's End O' Maine Kennels in Wisconsin) won or placed in the Sporting Group at the Garden every year but two. The Morris & Essex show was cancelled during part of WWII—1942-45—and in 1946, but in the five years it was held, these dogs won or placed in the group twice.

An article by Ross Howard (Far Flight Kennels in Boulder, Colorado) in the legendary September 1948 issue of *Popular Dog,* asks,

> *"What does the ideal English Setter look like?" Howard's answer was, "Say Jeff [Ch. Mallhawk Jeff, owned by C. N. Myers], say Rip [Ch. Rip of Blue Bar], mention Max [Ch. Sturdy Max], and Maro [Ch. Maro of Maridor]."*

While Ross Howard never owned a big winning English Setter, he certainly knew them when he saw them!

As the '40s drew to a close, English Setters were more competitive than ever in the show ring and a dominant force in AKC shows across the eastern and midwestern parts of the United States. The Blue Bar, Silvermine, Delwed, Maridor, and Prune's Own Kennels were producing stock that carried the "winning strain." Dog shows continued to gain in popularity all around the country, and more people were becoming involved. English Setters had been well represented by the dogs we have already met, but the best of the best had just begun to make his mark. And what a mark it was....

Endnotes

1. *AKC Gazettes*, 1938-43.

2. Ibid.

3. *Popular Dogs*, May 1943.

4. *AKC Gazettes*, 1939-45.

5. Ibid.

6. Ibid.

7. English Setter column, *AKC Gazette*, February 1946.

8. Priscilla St. George was first married to Angier Biddle Duke and was a well-known dog fancier and socialite as Mrs. A. Biddle Duke.

9. *AKC Gazettes*, 1944-46.

10. *AKC Gazettes*, 1940-50.

11. Ibid.

12. English Setter column, *AKC Gazette*, July 1948.

Chapter Four

The Golden Era, 1930-60: The 1950s

Climax of the Golden Era

1951 Morris & Essex K.C. Sporting Group—Ch. Rock Falls Colonel
(photo courtesy of St. Hubert's Animal Welfare Center, Madison N.J.)

The final decade of the golden era saw it all come together. The modern English Setter envisioned by Laverack and Llewellin; founded on Crombie, Mallwyd, and Selkirk; brought to America and formulated by Eric Bergishagen, J. J. Sinclair, Dr. A. A. Mitten, and A. J. Kruger; and fashioned into a winning breed by George Wedel, Charlie Palmer, C. N. Myers, Bill Holt, and Davis Tuck was about to reach a high-water mark. Blue Bar, Silvermine, and

Rock Falls enjoyed a "last hurrah" in producing some of the greatest show dogs of this decade. Riding the crest of the wave was the greatest English Setter show dog of all—*Ch. Rock Falls Colonel.*

Davis Tuck's book was written in 1950-51. In Chapter 14, he offered the following assessment:

> *Assuming that a mutation of all positive characteristics or a new prepotent sire is not found soon, I have analyzed the available stud dogs who, in my opinion, are capable of holding the good of the Mallwyd strain, and I list them in their order of merit, based on their get and their age. #1. Ch. Rock Falls Cavalier, age 4 yrs. W.T. Holt, Richmond Virginia.*

Those were prophetic words!

In 1937 Colonel and Mrs. William T. Holt's Rock Falls Kennels acquired a foundation stud dog, Ch. Grayland Racket's Boy—another outstanding son of the great Rummey Stagboro! Racket's Boy was selectively bred to C. N. Myers' Blue Bar stock (from Mallhawk Jeff) to produce Ch. Rock Falls Cavalier in 1946.

Then doubling up on the Rummey Stagboro side of their stock, in May 1948 the Holts whelped a litter with another pair of winning brothers, one of which would become the best English Setter of all time. *Ch. Rock Falls Colonel* began his show career at a little over one year of age in 1950. By the time he retired from the show ring in 1955, Colonel was the first dog in the history of AKC to have amassed *100 AKC Best in Shows.*[1] This was an unheard-of achievement in the dog world. What makes this accomplishment even more stunning was that throughout his show career the Colonel was handled by Bill Holt, his breeder-owner and hunting companion! The Colonel not only set the mark for Best in Shows; he set a new standard for showmanship. When he went *Best in Show* in *1951* at Morris & Essex, he was filmed by Quaker Oats for a promotional film. When he won the *Sporting Group at Westminster KC in 1952 (a win he repeated in 1956 at age eight)*, *The New York Times* reporter Court Page described the Best in Show and Group judging:

*Holt's English Setter, a superb animal, stood with his tail wagging incessantly....Sims [BIS Judge Joseph P. Sims] finished his close scrutiny and ordered each of the six, one by one; to strut the length of the green carpeted arena and back. **The Colonel Struts.**...Applause rattled through the Garden as Ch. Rock Falls Colonel strutted up the alley in his precision like gait.*

Although the Colonel retired for good shortly after the 1956 Westminster KC show, the May 1960 issue of the *AKC Gazette* included a tribute by Rebec Pusey, writing for the English Setter Association of America, in which she recounted that at a luncheon attended by one hundred English Setter breeders at the last Morris & Essex KC show in 1957, the Colonel was presented with a silver tray inscribed, "In honor of the retirement of Int. Ch. Rock Falls Colonel, the greatest show winning sporting dog of all times from the English Setter Breeders of America."[2] The Colonel can truly be called a dog show superstar!! Since greatness is measured not only by accomplishments but also by the competition, the Colonel and a boxer, Ch. Bangaway of Sirrah Crest, achieved their records of 100 BIS almost at the same time.

Ch. Rock Falls Colonel in Group (photo from archives of Gus Polley – Skidby)

The 1950s also saw the beginnings of National Ranking systems for show dogs. With the growth in the number of AKC-sanctioned dog shows and the increasing popularity of the sport, a way to compare the accomplishments of these superior animals was needed. The first company to develop a National Award System was the Quaker Oats Company, acting through its Ken-L-Ration dog food division. The "*Quaker Oats Awards*" were for the top dog in each AKC Group based upon the number of Group 1 wins earned during the show year. *Ch. Rock Falls Colonel won "Quaker Oats Sporting Group Dog" in three consecutive years, 1952, 1953, and 1954.* No other English Setter has ever done that. The Colonel's overall show record is truly staggering. Shown a total of 189 times, he went Best of Breed 173 times (*meaning he lost Best of Breed only 16 times in his entire life!!*). He won 162 Group firsts (an English Setter record lasting until 1990) and one hundred Best in Shows (still the English Setter record). While other English Setters have surpassed his Breed and Group totals, the Colonel's averages will probably never be equaled. His Group to Breed average is 93.6 percent; that is, he won the Sporting Group 93.6 percent of the times he won Best of Breed. His Best in Show to Breed average, 57.8 percent, is awesome: More than half the time he went Best of Breed, he went on to take Best in Show. In

Ch. Rock Falls Colonel (1951 advertisement from the author's collection)

fact, he went Best in Show in more than half the shows in which he was entered. It is an all but incredible record.

The many pictures of the Colonel all show the same thing, a great dog that provides another interpretation of the Standard. He was a richly colored, orange Belton of 26 inches and shown at 70 pounds. As you read the English Setter Standard, study the photos of the Colonel. In *The Complete Dog Book: An Official Publication of the AKC,* there are breed facts, standards, and a single photograph of a dog to illustrate that Standard.[3] The AKC chose Rock Falls Colonel to portray the English Setter Breed Standard. I was fortunate to obtain some old 8-mm. home movies that included about two minutes of Ch. Rock Falls Colonel running in his back yard. Judging by the cars in the background, it must have dated to around 1956, when he would have been eight years old. The ease and grace of his movement and the pure joy he exuded almost made me imagine he could do it again today. His was a greatness that never goes out of style.

The Colonel was not the only great English Setter show dog in the "fabulous '50s." Many more deserve mention. One was the Colonel's litter brother **Ch. Rock Falls Racket**, owned by Elsworth Howell.

Ch. Rock Falls Racket
(photo from archives of Bill and Lovey Trotter- Flecka's)

Shown by the incomparable Jane Kamp (Forsyth), he won the *1954 ESAA National Specialty* (from the Veteran's Class!) as well as **5 AKC BIS** between 1951 and 1954.[4] (A Challenge Trophy, the *Ch. Rock Falls Racket Trophy* was offered at the ESAA National until 1976, when the great Ch. Guys 'n Dolls Annie O'Brien retired and re-donated it, and was permanently retired in 1990 by the great Ch. Goodtime's Silk Teddy.) Racket and the Colonel were the latest pair of English Setter litter mates to rise to greatness in the show ring, following the example set by the Maridor and Delwed brothers.

C. N. Myers' **Blue Bar Kennels** reached its zenith in the 1940s and achieved its last great success in the early '50s. This included the first and only litter brother and sister to win ESAA National Specialties. *Ch. Sir Herbert of Kennelworth* (son of Rip of Blue Bar) won the 1950 ESAA National, and the winner of the *1951 ESAA National*, was his *litter sister, Ch. Miss Frivolous*. Another of C. N. Myers' Blue Bar dogs, *Ch. Ludar of Blue Bar* (son of Sir Herbert of Kennelworth), won *13 AKC BIS* between 1950 and 1954,[5] and this while competing against the Rock Falls brothers. And Blue Bar's winning ways continued after Myers' death in 1954. *Ch. Ike of Blue Bar* (son of Rock Falls Racket) won *back-to-back ESAA Nationals in 1955 and 1956* as well as *7 AKC BIS* between 1954 and 1957.[6] An article in the *1968 ESAA Annual* describes the man who had as much impact on the breed in the United States as did A. A. Mitten, A. J. Kruger, Eric Bergishagen, and others before him. Blue Bar dogs won 8 ESAA Nationals (with six different dogs) and 36 BIS (among five different dogs) between 1939 and 1957.

Ch. Sir Herbert of Kennelworth
   (photo courtesy of Dr. Carl Sillman, ESAA Historian)

Ch. Miss Frivolous
   (photo courtesy of Dr. Carl Sillman, ESAA Historian)

Ch. Ludar of Blue Bar

(*photo from archives of Gus Polley – Skidby*)

Ch. Ike of Blue Bar

(*photo courtesy of Dr. Carl Sillman, ESAA Historian*)

Davis and Virginia Tuck's ***Ch. Silvermine Whipcord*** (a Wagabond grandson) won the ***ESAA National in 1952***. Virginia Tuck became the ***first owner-handler to win three ESAA Nationals***. Like C. N. Myers, the Tucks provided foundation stock to many kennels of English Setters to come, and Davis' book *The Complete English Setter* remains the guide to the lineage of the great English Setters.

Ch. Silvermine Whipcord
 (photo from archives of Gus Polley – Skidby)

Handled by his owner, William T. Holt, ***Ch. Rock Falls Skyway*** (son of Rock Falls Colonel) won the ***ESAA National in 1953*** and was the last English Setter to win a ***Group 1 at Morris & Essex in 1953***.

Ch. Rock Falls Skyway 1953 Morris & Essex K.C. Sporting Group (photo courtesy of St. Hubert's Animal

Ch. Chatterwood on the Rocks (a Rock Falls Racket son) made his bid for glory in an all too brief career. Handled by his owner, Dr. Raymond Chase, and Jane Kamp (Forsyth), he won *back-to-back ESAA Nationals in 1957 and 1958.* In a career cut short when he was struck and killed by a car in December 1958, this magnificent Setter won *7 BISS* in a time when there were only four or five Specialties in the entire year![7] English Setter trivia fans will recall that Ch. Chatterwood on the Rocks went second in Group at the last Morris & Essex KC show in 1957.

1956 E.S.C. N.E. Specialty – Best of Breed judging. Ch. Chatterwood on the Rocks is the second dog from the right

In 1956 another national ranking system was inaugurated. Developed and managed by the late Irene Castle Phillips Khatoonian Schlintz, the *Phillips System* recorded the number of competitors each dog defeated at the Breed, Group, and Best in Show levels. Dogs were ranked at the Breed, Group, and All-Breed levels based on the cumulative number of dogs defeated during the year. Published from 1956 to 1991, it indicates the relative success of English Setters (and all other breeds) at each level of competition. The Phillips System made it possible to determine how English Setters compared to each other, to top Sporting dogs, and to top dogs in all breeds. It shows that English Setters did well indeed.

Ch. Yorkley Ensign Roberts
> *(photo from archives of Gus Polley – Skidby)*

   Ch. Yorkley Ensign Roberts (a Rip of Blue Bar grandson) was the *No. 10* dog in the Sporting Group in *1956* with 11 Group 1s and a BIS. Yorkley Kennels, owned by John Stocker, was prominent in the Midwest during the 1950s. An ESAA Annual award, *The Yorkley Award*, is presented to the breeder of the BISS winner at the ESAA National Specialty.

   Marge O'Connell (more widely known for her *Hiddenlane* Kennels) actually began her influence on the breed by teaming up with Bill Sears, the owner of Ch. Ludar of Blue Bar. They purchased a bitch from Davis Tuck (Ch. Silvermine Chambray) and formed the *Ben-Dar* Kennels.[9] Marge and Bill bred many winning Ben-Dar setters during the '50s and '60s, but their best was *Ch. Ben Dar's Winning Stride* (a Ludar of Blue Bar son, bred by John Stocker but whelped by Marge in her home). Stride, handled by Hayden "Doc" Martin, was the *No. 4 Sporting Group* dog in *1958* with *6 Group 1s* and *2 BIS*.[10] In a famous photograph taken at the Detroit KC show in 1958, we can see the fruits of Marge and Bill's efforts. A copy of this photograph remains in the wallet of Chuck Herendeen, handler of Ch. Ben-Dar's Replica and now an AKC judge. Stride and the Ben-Dar line would go on to become important foundations for her famous Hiddenlane Kennels of the '70s.

Ch. Ben Dar's Winning Stride
  (photo from archives of Bill and Lovey Trotter- Flecka's)

Closing out the decade in 1959 was ***Ch. Zamitz Jumping Jack*** (a tri-color grandson of Rock Falls Racket), handled by Robert Forsyth, winning the ***1959 ESAA National*** and the first of his ***6 BIS***.[11] Jumping Jack was ranked ***No. 4 in the Sporting Group*** by the Phillips System in ***1959*** with 13 Group 1s and 5 BIS. Within the breed, he is still the top-winning BIS and BISS tri-color English Setter.

Ch. Zamitz Jumpin' Jack
  (photo from archives of Gus Polley – Skidby)

LUDAR and his get:
Left to Right:
AM/CAN CH. DARBY OF CARYLANE
AM/CAN CH. BEN-DAR'S REPLICA
With Chuck Herendeen
AM/CAN CH. LUDAR OF BLUE BAR
With Horace Hollands
AM/CAN CH. BEN-DAR'S ADVANCE NOTICE
AM/CAN CH. BEN-DAR'S WINNING STRIDE
AM/CAN CH. BEN-DAR'S CARBON COPY
CH. BEN-DAR' SWEET SUE

Ben-Dar Family (photo from archives of Bill and Lovey Trotter- Flecka's)

Using all the National Ranking systems in place in the 1950s, English Setters were well accounted for. They were No. 1 in Sporting Group in 1951, 1952, and 1953, No. 10 in 1956, and No. 4 in 1958 and 1959.

With the passing of Clinton N. Myers (Blue Bar) and Davis Tuck (Silvermine) and the retirement of Bill Holt (Rock Falls), the day of the large English Setter breeding kennels came to an end. The prohibitive cost of land and other economic factors made breeding kennels on the scale of Happy Valley, Rock Falls, Mallhawk, and

Maridor impossible to sustain. The breed was now in the hands of the hobby or show kennel, where a smaller and more selective breeding program was the rule. The "winning strain" would continue, but it would now include names like Ben-Dar, Chandelle, Flecka's, Margand, Manlove, Skidby, Stone Gables, and Valley Run.

Endnotes

1. *AKC Gazettes, 1948-57.*

2. Int. Ch. Rock Falls Colonel was also a Cuban Champion finishing with a Cuban Best in Show. In the 1950s this was enough to qualify for the designation of an International Champion (Int. Ch.). The criteria for an International Champion are different today. This Cuban Best in Show was added to the Colonel's totals in advertisements, and he was listed as having 101 Best in Shows. For this book we count only the Colonel's one hundred AKC Best in Shows.

3. *The Complete Dog Book, an official publication of the AKC, 1968.*

4. *AKC Gazettes, 1948-59.*

5. Ibid.

6. Ibid.

7. Ibid.

8. *Setters, Inc.*, June/July 1986.

9. *AKC Gazettes*, 1957-61.

10. Ibid.

Chapter Five

The 1960's—Spread the Wealth!

*Ch. Chandelle's
Anchor Man
(head study)*

*(photo from
archives of
Marsha Hall
Brown)*

As the 1960s dawned, the "winning strain" was present in many English Setter kennels. The great Mallwyd dogs, Rummey Stagboro and Sturdy Max, passed the strain to Blue Bar, Rock Falls, and Silvermine. They in turn distributed it to many of the small show kennels of the 1960s. English Setters had been a dominant force in the Sporting Group and All-Breed levels for thirty years. Between 1930 and 1959, English Setters won or placed in the Sporting Group at the Westminster KC in nineteen of thirty shows. They won or placed in the Sporting Group at the Morris & Essex KC 13 times between 1930 and 1957, when that show ended. We now chronicle the dogs of the 1960s who carried on this tradition and the "winning strain."

The English Setter first to rise to national prominence in the '60s was Andrew and Margaret Hawn's **Ch. Margand Lord Baltimore.** Shown by Dick Cooper, this grandson of Rock Falls Colonel won 5 **AKC BIS** and **4 Specialty BISS** between 1959 and 1962[1] and, appropriately enough, the ESAA's **Rock Falls Colonel Award** for the most BIS in **1961**. Elsworth Howell acclaimed Lord Baltimore in his June 1962 column in *Popular Dogs*:

> *Lord Baltimore has amassed a considerable record under Dick Cooper's excellent handling for the Andrew Hawns, his owner-breeders. At this writing* [June 1962], *he has 100 BOB's, 27 GP1's and 5 BIS. His batting average in group placements is .720, a remarkable achievement in any Setter league.*

This "batting average" means that one hundred Best of Breed victories led to seventy-two Sporting Group placings. Lord Baltimore began the decade of the '60s by continuing the strong presence of English Setters in the Group and Best in Show rings.

Ch. Margand Lord Baltimore
        (photo from archives of Bill and Lovey Trotter- Flecka's)

Following on his heels was Jeanne Millet's ***Ch. Candlewood Distinction*** (an Ike of Blue Bar son) owned by Mrs. Cheever Porter, a renowned dog fancier from New York City. During the first half of the 1960s, Candlewood Distinction, shown by Jane Kamp (Forsyth), won the ***1963 and 1965 ESAA National Specialties***; was ***ESAA Dog of the Year*** and ***Rock Falls Colonel winner in 1962, 1963, and 1964***; and was ranked (by the Phillips System) among the top ten dogs in the ***Sporting Group for 1962 (No. 10), 1963 (No. 9), and 1964 (No. 1)***. Distinction was featured on the cover of the March 1964 issue of *Popular Dogs,* and in that same month won five consecutive Sporting Groups in less than one week! Between 1960 and 1964, Distinction won ***7 AKC BIS*** and a total of ***6 BISS***, and he retired at the Garden in 1965 with a BOB/GP3.[2]

Ch. Candlewood Distinction w/ Jane Kamp
(photo from archives of Gus Polley – Skidby)

The great English Setters have always had great competition. Candlewood Distinction's strong and handsome rival in the English Setter Specialty ring was ***Ch. Flecka's Flash of Cabin Hill*** (another grandson of Rock Falls Colonel), bred by Bill and Lovey Trotter,

initially owned by Rebec and Van Pusey (Cabin Hill), and later sold
to Mrs. Sidney Smith of Bayonet Point Kennels. These two great
English Setters battled in ESAA's National Specialty ring for four
straight years. Flecka's Flash began with a win at the *1962 ESAA
National* and reclaimed the National's crown with a second victory at
the *1964 ESAA National Specialty.* Flash, handled by Rebec Pusey
and later by famous sporting dog handler Art Bains, won a total of *6
BISS.*[3] Competition among English Setters was never more intense
than in the early 1960s.

Ch. Flecka's Flash of Cabin Hill
        (photo from archives of Bill and Lovey Trotter- Flecka's)

Other notable English Setters from the early 1960s include Pete
and Gus Polley's *Ch. Skidby's Sturdy Tyke*, a Ludar of Blue Bar grand-
son. Sturdy Tyke was an AKC *BIS* dog who won the *ESAA Rock Falls
Colonel Award* (for most BIS in a year) in *1958* and the *1960 ESAA
National.* This beautiful light orange male from the Polley's famous
Skidby Kennels in Canada had the honor of winning the National
Specialty at the inaugural Combined Setter Clubs show in New York
in 1960, where he was judged by Mrs. Geraldine Dodge (of Morris
& Essex fame).

Ch. Skidby's Sturdy Tyke
(photo from archives of Bill and Lovey Trotter- Flecka's)

Also in the 1960s, Rachael and Dutch Van Buren's Valley Run Kennels produced a number of notable English Setters, which were handled by Robert Forsyth. The first of these, ***Ch. English Accent of Valley Run*** (a Rock Falls Racket son), won the ***ESAA National in 1961***, was ***ESAA Dog of the Year in 1960***, and won ***3 BISS*** between 1960 and 1961.[4]

Ch. English Accent of Valley Run
(photo from archives of Gus Polley – Skidby)

The Trotters' ***Ch. Flecka's Charlie***, a litter brother to Ch. Flecka's Flash of Cabin Hill (here we have another pair of winning brothers), owned by Paul and Ann Billingsley, won *5 BISS* between 1960 and 1962 in the Pacific Northwest.[5]

As the halfway mark of the decade approached, two dogs were born who were destined to make their mark. In the Midwest, Warren Brewbaker bred ***Ch. Chandelle's Anchor Man***, a son of Lord Baltimore, and thus a perpetuator of the "winning strain." "Balty" and his owner-handler Joe Kaziny began to win "right from the get go." In his *Popular Dogs* column report on the 1962 International KC show in June 1962, Elsworth Howell noted:

> *At the great International K.C. show in Chicago, Ch. Margand Lord Baltimore topped his illustrious show career with a GP1 and saw his **10-month old son**, Joseph Kaziny's **Anchor Man** take Best of Winners, in a 4-point entry.*

Ch. Chandelle's Anchor Man
　　　　　(*photo from archives of Marsha Hall Brown*)

When "Balty" began his specials career, he continued to win at the Group and All-Breed level with *6 AKC BIS*, and dominated at the Specialty level with an *incredible 23 Specialty BISS between 1963 and 1970.*[6] *Anchor Man holds the absolute record among English Setters for the number of Specialty bests, with 5 more than his nearest rival.* Anchor Man won the *1967 ESAA National Specialty* and was selectively exhibited after his retirement until the age of twelve! Warren Brewbaker has the distinction of being the *first English Setter breeder to have a full litter brother and sister win both Best of Breed and Best of Opposite Sex at the* **same** *ESAA National Specialty.* Joining Anchor Man on the winner's podium at the 1967 ESAA National was his litter sister Ch. Chandelle's Bambi.

Ch. Chandelle's Anchor Man & Ch. Chandelle's Bambi – BISS and BOS at 1965 ESAA National Specialty.
(photo from archives of Marsha Hall Brown)

Bill and Lovey Trotter (Flecka English Setters) tell an interesting anecdote about Anchor Man.[7] Early in his show career, Brewbaker and Kaziny flew him to California to attend the famous Santa Barbara KC show, at the time the largest AKC show in the United States. Bill and Lovey met Joe and were recommending grooming techniques for Anchor Man. Joe, never shy, demanded to know what

Ch. Chandelle's Anchor Man in Group
　　　　(photo from archives of Bill and Lovey Trotter- Flecka's)

brand of thinning shears they intended to use. When they gave the "correct" answer, they were permitted to groom Anchor Man. This "California technique" would remain with the dog for the rest of his career. (A remarkably similar incident occurred years later with Ch. Goodtime's Silk Teddy.)

While Anchor Man was the terror of the Midwest shows and all the Specialties, ***Ch. Merry Rover of Valley Run***, a Rock Falls Racket grandson, made his presence felt in the East. Shown by William Trainor for his owners, Rachael Van Buren and Mrs. George Abbot, Merry Rover won ***10 AKC BIS*** and ***8 BISS***, including the ***1966 ESAA Nationals, between 1965 and 1968.***[8] He was ***ESAA Dog of the Year in 1966*** and won the ***Rock Falls Colonel Award in 1965, 1966, and 1967***. Merry Rover was the ***No. 4 dog in the Sporting Group in 1965***, according to the Phillips System.

In the third edition of Davis Tuck's *The Complete English Setter*, Elsworth Howell comments on the dogs he has seen and judged. In his chapter on "Leading Winners of the 1950's and 1960's" he writes:

Ch. Merry Rover of Valley Run
            (photo from archives of Gus Polley – Skidby)

> *Anchor Man and Merry Rover dominated the English*
> *Setter scene in 1965 and 1966 with substantial Group,*
> *Specialty and BIS wins. I judged both of these magnifi-*
> *cent specimens a number of times, once together when the*
> *decision was the closest and most difficult I have ever*
> *adjudicated. In their prime they, and Ch. Chatterwood*
> *on the Rocks, represented—in my opinion—the finest*
> *English Setters of the past 20 years. (In fact, I tried*
> *mightily to acquire each!)*

Merry Rover retired in 1967, but his place in the continuum of
the "winning strain" was admirably taken by ***Ch. Sir Kip of Manitou***[9]
Sir Kip (sired by Ch. Skidby's Bosun of Stone Gables) has lines that
include Rock Falls Racket, Blue Bar, and all the way back to Sturdy
Max. Bred by Richard Howe of Clariho Kennels and owned by Stan
and Beth Silverman, Sir Kip was piloted to his championship by
Marsha Hall Brown (with three 5-point Specialty majors) and campaigned by William Trainor. Sir Kip was a multiple BIS winner who
also won ***12 BISS***, including the ***1968 and 1969 ESAA National
Specialties.*** He won ***ESAA's Dog of the Year in 1968 and 1969.***[10]

Ch. Sir Kip of Manitou with owner Stan Silverman
(photo courtesy of Silverman family)

Another milestone in the show history of English Setters was established in the '60s by a beautiful lightly marked orange Belton bitch, **Ch. Canberra's Legend**. A Rock Falls Racket granddaughter bred by the legendary W. F. Gilroy (see Ch. Gilroy's Chief Topic in the 1930s)[11], owned by Dr. and Mrs. George (Joyce) Rosen, and owner-handled by Joyce, Legend won **3 AKC BIS** in 1970 and was the first English Setter Bitch to win **ESAA's Rock Falls Colonel Award** (in 1970). This beautiful bitch won a total of **6 BISS between 1968 and 1970**,[12] and today, one of ESAA's most cherished Annual Awards is the *Canberra's Legend Award,* presented to the English Setter bitch winning the most AKC Best in Shows during the year.

The Midwest saw another descendant of the winning strain in **Ch. Baker's Northern Lancer** (great-grandson of Rock Falls Colonel). Lance was a stunningly impressive orange Belton dog, winning many Groups and **3 BISS** for his owner-handler Dave Baker **between 1968 and 1969**.[13] Among the first English Setter breeders my wife and I met were Fran and Ben Sprecher of Pleasant Point kennels. They owned Ch. Rock Falls Lieutenant and bred Northern Lancer. One of Ben's stories (which he has told again and again) was how he went out of town on a business trip and told Fran *not* to sell one particular

Ch. Canberra's Legend
            (photo from archives of Marsha Hall Brown)

Ch. Baker's Northern Lancer
            (photo from archives of Marsha Hall Brown)

puppy. Fran, as the listener soon guesses, failed to follow those instructions and sold *that one puppy* to Dave Baker. This was Baker's Northern Lancer, and Ben was ultimately pleased with the success Dave Baker had.

The "winning strain" that Davis Tuck had so astutely identified was now widely dispersed throughout English Setters in America. The qualities that led to the success of the direct descendents of Rummey Stagboro, Ch. Sturdy Max, the Maridor and Delwed brothers, and the dogs of Blue Bar and Rock Falls would now be found in grandsons and great-grandsons who carried this strain. And as the decade of the 1960s drew to a close, new show kennels like Clairho, Hiddenlanes, Manlove, and Guys 'n Dolls made their presence known.

Endnotes

1. *AKC Gazettes, 1958-63.*

2. AKC Gazettes, 1960-63.

3. Ibid.

4. Ibid.

5. Ibid.

6. AKC Gazettes, 1961-71.

7. Bill and Lovey Trotter, interview, December 2001.

8. AKC Gazettes, 1964-69.

9. Sir Kip was also a Canadian and Bermudan champion.

10. AKC Gazettes, 1966-70.

11. William F. Gilroy owned Clover Ridge Kennels and was the breeder of Ch. Gilroy's Chief Topic, one of the famous English Setters mentioned in this book.

12. AKC Gazettes, 1968-71.

13. Ibid.

Chapter Six

The 1970s—Go West Young Man!

From the 1930s through the 1960s, the development and campaigning of English Setters in America was largely confined to the East and Midwest. This reflected the historical beginnings of the breed. To be sure, there were such notable exceptions as A. J. Kruger's Mallhawk kennels in Oregon, J. J. Sinclair's Orkney Kennels in California, and Norm McConnell's Selkirk kennels in Vancouver, British Columbia. But by 1970, English Setters were widely distributed around the country, and many show kennels established in California in the '50s and '60s had begun to produce very significant Setters. Of these, the most notable was the Guys 'n Dolls Kennel of Neal Weinstein. Neal used stock from two Canadian kennels, Gus Polley's Skidby Kennels and the Hillsdale Kennels (which doubled on the Ludar of Blue Bar lineage), to begin his line. In 1968 Neal had finished and was showing a striking male, *Ch. Guys 'n Dolls Shalimar Duke*, the first in a long list of Guys 'n Dolls dogs and bitches to carry on the winning tradition. Duke was an evenly marked orange Belton with a depth of color to his ticking and a magnificent headpiece. Shown by Dick Webb, the Duke won *6 AKC BIS* and *8 BISS between 1968 and 1971*,[1] including the *1970 ESAA National*. He was *ESAA's Dog of the Year in 1970 and 1971* and was the *Rock Falls Colonel Award* winner in *1971*. By the Phillips System rankings, Shalimar Duke was the

No. 10 Sporting dog in 1969 and *No. 2 in Group in 1970.* The Duke was also a dominant sire, with seventy-six Champion get (third most champions sired by an English Setter).

Ch. Guys 'n Dolls Shalimar Duke
(photo from archives of Gus Polley – Skidby)

The climb to success by the Setters of Guys 'n Dolls (and most notably their bitches) had just begun. Neal bred Shalimar Duke to a Rock Falls Colonel granddaughter and produced another preeminent male, *Ch. Guys 'n Dolls Onassis.* Onassis, also shown by Dick Webb, was a *Best in Show* winner that also won *4 BISS between 1971 and 1976.*[2] He was bred to another of Neal's bitches in 1971 and produced a truly legendary bitch.

In 1973, at only twenty months of age, *Ch. Guys 'n Dolls Annie O'Brien* went Best of Opposite Sex (BOS) at the ESAA National. It is worth noting that on that same day, Ch. Hiddenlane's Benchmark went BISS under Judge Elsworth Howell, and, as we shall later see, this foretold great things from these two kennels. Over the next three years, Annie O'Brien, owned by Lloyd and Linda Talbot, went on to become one of the greatest English Setters in history. She was the first English Setter (and one of only two) to win *3 ESAA National Specialty BISS*, and she won them *consecutively in 1974, 1975,* and

1976. Annie O'Brien also won *13 AKC BIS* plus a total of *9 BISS* in her career, a record for bitches that stood for thirteen years.[3] Especially impressive about Annie's 9 Specialty BISS is that three were Nationals and two were Combined Setter Clubs of America. Annie was the prettiest puppy anyone could hope for. Even at four months of age her face markings were clearly dazzling. Later, she grew to "have it all."[4] Equally imposing was her ring presence; she was a show dog in the truest sense of the word. Her flair was something not seen since the Colonel himself, and she taught the English Setter world of the '70s the value of that indefinable quality "spirit." In an article for the *1994 ESAA Annual*, Annie's handler, Ray McGinnis, said of her, "The first thing that comes to mind is that Annie was unique—different than most English Setter bitches. In temperament she was, above all, a show dog."

Ch. Guys 'n Dolls Annie O'Brien w/ Lloyd Talbot
(photo courtesy of Garth Gourlay archives)

Annie won *ESAA Dog of the Year in 1975* and the *Rock Falls Colonel Award in 1974 and 1975*, and was ranked *No. 3 in the Sporting Group* by the Phillips System in *1974* (that year she won 10 BIS). A beautiful ESAA award, The Guys 'n Dolls Annie O'Brien Award (featuring a colored bronze of Annie), is now presented to the bitch winning Best of Breed or Best of Opposite at the ESAA National. My wife and I were fortunate to have our Ch. Goodtime's Silk Teddy win this beautiful award and to keep it in our home for three years.

While Annie was making breed history, more Guys 'n Dolls bitches claimed the '70s for their own. In 1976 *Ch. Guys 'n Dolls Taste of Honey* (another Shalimar Duke daughter) was *ESAA Dog of the Year* and shared in a four-way tie for the *Rock Falls Colonel Award* for Best in Shows. Shown by William Trainor for her owner David Ruml, she also won *6 BISS between 1976 and 1979*[5] as well as BOS at the 1979 ESAA National. Jodelle Burke's *Ch. Guys 'n Dolls Rosa Midnight* (a Shalimar Duke daughter) won *5 BISS between 1973 and 1977*.[6] Guys 'n Dolls bitches were as strong a show and breeding force, in their day, as had been those from the famous Blue Bar Kennels of C. N. Myers. And like C. N., Neal accorded them equal status in the ring. The dedication inscribed on the Ch. Guys 'n Dolls Annie O'Brien Award reads as follows: "In special tribute to all the bitches throughout English Setter history, truly the foundation of the breed." Neal, like C. N. Myers and other top breeders, understood the importance of bitches.

Ch. Guys 'n Dolls Rosa Midnight
(photo from archives of Gus Polley – Skidby)

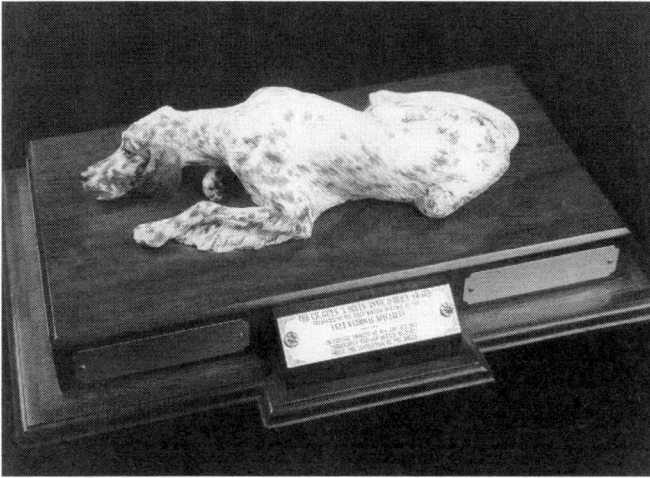

Annie O'Brien Award Trophy (from the author's collection)

Closing out the decade, ***Ch. Guys n' Dolls Wild William*** (another Shalimar Duke son) was ***ESAA Dog of the Year in 1979*** and ***No. 10 in the Sporting Group*** in the Phillips System. Owned by Jerry and Betty Olive, William was shown by Ray McGinnis, who had a special affinity with English Setters, and Guys 'n Dolls dogs in particular.

California Setters continued to make their presence felt in the 1970s. Charles and Linda Sullivan's ***Ch. Charlin Rudolph*** (an Onassis son), shown by Corky Vroom, was ***ESAA Dog of the Year*** and a tie winner of the ***Rock Falls Colonel Award in 1973.*** "Rudy" won ***2 AKC BIS*** and ***3 BISS between 1973 and 1978.***[7] ***Ch. Sunburst Special Edition***, sired by Shalimar Duke, bred by Yvonne Ward and Joan Solheim, and shown by co-owner Bruce Shultz, won the ***1977 ESAA National Specialty.*** And the following year, ***Ch. Storybooks Best Seller*** (a Shalimar Duke grandson) won the ***1978 ESAA National***; he was ***ESAA Dog of the Year in 1977 and 1978.*** Shown in the Midwest by Dick Cooper for his owner, Chuck Prieb, Best Seller had ***3 BISS*** in his show career.[8]

Lest the reader think that in the 1970s English Setters were bred only in California, it should be noted that other kennels had (and continue to have) a major impact on the breed. They were found in the Midwest, including one state in particular, Michigan, which was always home to great English Setters. Led by Eric Bergishagen's

Ch. Storybooks Best Seller (photo from archives of Marsha Hall Brown)

Jagersbo kennels and George Wedel's Delwed dogs, English Setter breeders in Michigan have produced quality dogs and nurtured the "winning strain." By the beginning of the 1970s, Marge O'Connell's Ben-Dar line had evolved into Hiddenlane Kennels, and her *Ch. Hiddenlane's Merry Max* (a Winning Stride grandson) was a top show English between *1970 and 1973*. Merry Max was a *multiple BIS winner* who also won *3 BISS*, including the *1971 ESAA National Specialty*.[9] Continuing a line that went back to C. N. Myers's Blue Bar and Davis Tuck's Silvermine stock, Marge bred another top Hiddenlane dog, *Ch. Hiddenlane's Benchmark*, a Blue Turquoise son, owned by Robert and Jackie Anderson, who did justice to his lineage by garnering *5 BISS* between 1973 and 1976, including the *1973 ESAA National, as well as 3 AKC BIS*.[10] He was among four English tied for the *Rock Falls Colonel Award in 1976*.

Many more Hiddenlane setters were highly competitive in the 1970s, most notably a beautiful orange Belton bitch, *Ch. Hiddenlane Special Delivery*, a Blue Turquoise granddaughter owned by Bob and Mary Nelson who won *5 BISS between 1977 and 1980*.[11]

The "winning strain" in other midwestern kennels produced more great dogs in the 1970s. An Anchor Man son, *Ch. Sukarla's Sandpiper*, bred by John Nielsen and owned by Erv and Mary Ciszek of Barrington, Illinois, won the *1972 ESAA National*.

Ch. Hiddenlane's Benchmark
            (photo from archives of Gus Polley – Skidby)

Ch. Briarpatch of Bryn Mawr, a vivid open-marked tri-color male bred and owned by Ralph and Mary Wendels of Fond du Lac, Wisconsin, won *5 AKC BIS between 1973 and 1974.*[12] As a friend of Ralph Wendels, I saw "Patch" take one of his BIS in 1974. He was the most beautiful tri I have ever seen and never put a foot down wrong. Patch was tied for the ESAA *Rock Falls Colonel Award in 1973* (with Ch. Charlin' Rudolph) and again in *1974* (with Annie O'Brien).

Dave Baker followed the show success of his Ch. Bakers Northern Lancer with a bitch of his own breeding, ***Ch. Burr Ridge Constellation.*** "Connie" was a beautiful orange who won *4 BISS* in just two years, *1976 and 1977*, and went BOS at the 1977, 1978, and 1981 ESAA National Specialties to crown a fine show career.[13]

Despite all the excitement in the West and Midwest, eastern Setters were by no means absent from the show ring. In *1972 Ch. Highland's Whip of Penmaen*, an evenly marked blue Belton (with Yorkley, Blue Bar, Shiplake, and Silvermine lineage) owned by Susan Maire,[14] won the *ESAA Dog of the Year* and *Rock Falls Colonel Awards*. Whip also won *3 BISS* between 1971 and 1973.[15]

Ch. Briarpatch of Bryn Mawr
(photo courtesy of Garth Gourlay archives)

Ch. Burr Ridge Constellation
(photo from archives of Marsha Hall Brown)

Ch. Highland's Whip of Penmaen
  (photo from archives of Gus Polley – Skidby)

Margaret McCleary's ***Ch. Guyline's Flying Tiger*** (a Sir Kip son), bred by David and Shelia Ben-Hur, won ***4 BISS in 1971 and 1972***.[16] Another beautiful male, ***Ch. Arundel's Duke of Norfolk*** (a Sir Kip grandson), was a consistent breed winner and was the ***ESAA Dog of the Year in 1974***. Duke also won ***3 BISS between 1973 and 1975***.[17]

Ch. Guyline's Flying Tiger
  (photo courtesy of Garth Gourlay archives)

Ch. Arundel's Duke of Norfolk
(photo from archives of Gus Polley – Skidby)

Dogs from the Clariho Kennels of Sally and Dick Howe and part-ner Jane Slosson continued to do well in the English Setter Specialty ring, with ***Ch. Clariho Kristofer of Critt-du*** (a Shalimar Duke son) and his son ***Ch. Clariho Knight Rider*** each winning ***3 BISS***. In a Summer 1981 interview in *The Setter Quarterly*, Sally Howe said that her aim was to breed dogs that would win at Specialties. She clearly met that goal with her three best specials—Sir Kip, Kristofer, and Knight Rider—winning a combined 18 Specialty BISS ribbons.

Ch. Clariho Kristofer of Critt-du
(photo from archives of Gus Polley – Skidby)

The decade ended with an eastern Setter, **Ch. Velvet's Blue Moon** (a Whip of Penmaen son), winning the **1979 ESAA National Specialty.** This handsome male, in vivid blue and white with orange markings, bred by Richard and Judith White and owned by Sarah Sly, was only the second tri-color English Setter to win the ESAA National Specialty (the great Zamitz Jumpin' Jack being the first). He also won a total of **5 BISS between 1978 and 1981.**[18]

Ch. Velvet's Blue Moon
(photo courtesy of Garth Gourlay archives)

Once again it might be well for the reader to pause, possibly reread the chapter, and think about its meaning. The twenty English Setters mentioned in this chapter together account *for all the ESAA National Specialties winners, over 30 AKC BIS, and more than 90 Separate Specialty BISS.* Of those twenty, half (less only Shalimar Duke himself) were either sired by the great Shalimar Duke or were his grandchildren! The first three-time ESAA Nationals winner (Annie O'Brien) and three of the top ten sires in breed history were Guys 'n Dolls Setters bred by Neal Weinstein.[19]

Two ESAA Nationals and another 3 BIS and 13 BISS were won by Marge O'Connell's Hiddenlane dogs. If you include Marge's famous Ben-Dar dogs, the "winning strain" was clearly alive and well in the stock of Guys 'n Dolls and Hiddenlane. As we move into the decade of the 1980s, bloodlines of these two great kennels will combine to produce one of the greatest winning English Setters of all time.

Endnotes

1. *AKC Gazettes*, 1967-72.

2. *AKC Gazettes*, 1970-77.

3. Ibid.

4. Marsha Hall Brown, interview, December 2001.

5. *AKC Gazettes*, 1974-80.

6. *AKC Gazettes*, 1972-79.

7. Ibid.

8. *AKC Gazettes*, 1977-81.

9. *AKC Gazettes*, 1969-74.

10. *AKC Gazettes*, 1972-77.

11. *AKC Gazettes*, 1976-81.

12. *AKC Gazettes*, 1972-75.

13. *AKC Gazettes*, 1975-78.

14. Ibid.

15. Susan Maire is the author of the 1964 book *How to Raise and Train an English Setter.*

16. *AKC Gazettes*, 1970-76.

17. Ibid.

18. *AKC Gazettes*, 1977-82.

19. The three sires of English Setter AKC Champions are No. 3. Ch. Guys 'n Dolls Shalimar Duke; No. 5. Ch. Guys 'n Dolls Barrister Beau; and No. 6. Ch. Guys 'n Dolls Onassis. See Table 9 in the Appendixes for the complete list.

Chapter Seven

The 1980s—Back in the High Life

Ch. Goodtime's Silk Teddy: Best of Breed judging Westminister K.C.
(photo by Chet Jezierski from the author's collection)

In spite of all their accomplishments in the 1970s, English Setters were notably absent from the Best in Show ring in the last half of the decade. Shalimar Duke, Annie O'Brien, Benchmark, and Briarpatch had done their BIS winning in the early 1970s, and the later years were almost barren. The 1980s saw the beginning of a resurgence of English Setter show dogs at the Sporting Group and All-Breed level and would culminate with the greatest trio since the Rock Falls brothers and Ludar of Blue Bar in the early 1950s.

The period began with two Setters on the West Coast. *Ch. Lorien's American Flyer* (a Shalimar Duke grandson bred by Jeff and Irene Bottrell), owned by Betta Kaiser and shown by Tom Tobin, won *ESAA Dog of the Year in 1980* and finished his career with *4 BISS*.[1]

Meanwhile, yet another Guys 'n Dolls bitch, *Ch. Guys 'n Dolls Molly Bloom* (an Onassis granddaughter), owned by Tracy Marks, won the *1980 ESAA National Specialty*. Earlier, she had won the *1976 ESAA Futurity*, a special show for young dogs, many of whom have gone on to successful Specials careers. In the 1976 Futurity, the first held since WWII, Molly Bloom carried on a tradition begun by famous dogs such as Maro of Maridor, winner of the 1938 Futurity.

On the East Coast, David Ruml and I. F. Zimmerman's *Ch. Drummont's Tasty's Billy* (a Shalimar Duke grandson and son of their Ch. Guys 'n Dolls Taste of Honey) began his winning ways under the handling of Bill Trainor. After winning the *ESAA Futurity in 1979*, Tasty's Billy went on to make his mark, winning the *ESAA National Specialty in 1981* and *ESAA's Dog of the Year and Rock Falls Colonel Awards in both 1981 and 1982*. His finest year was 1982. He won the *Sporting Group at the Westminster KC* show (the last English Setter to do so) and was the *No. 3 Sporting dog in 1982* in the Phillips System. Billy retired in 1983 with a career total of *7 BIS and 10 BISS*, the fifth-best Specialty total in English Setter history.[2]

Also in *1982*, Canadians Jim and Carol Knudsen's *Ch. Ebb Tide's Me and My Shadow* (an Onassis grandson) tasted glory, winning the *ESAA National Specialty* from the classes. Herb Johnson's *Ch. Bricton Reau's High Tide* (from a Stone Gables dam) had a wonderful run in the early 1980s and finished his career with *4 BISS* and a *BIS between 1980 and 1983*.[3]

In the East, Colonel and Mrs. Robert Stevens' Fieldplay Kennels began to produce the foundations for the continuation of "the winning strain." Their *Ch. Windem's Lotsa Dots*, a beautiful blue Belton bitch with strong Clariho background, bred and shown by Jack Gohde, won the *ESAA National in 1983* and went on to a fine career including *3 BISS*.[4] "Dot" was bred to Ch. Guys 'n Dolls Barrister Beau (a BIS winner and son of the great Annie O' Brien) to produce

Ch. Ebb Tide's Me and My Shadow
            (photo courtesy of Garth Gourlay archives)

the foundation dog (Ch. Fieldplay's Set'r Ridge Jahil) for the renowned Set'r Ridge Kennels. Fieldplay Setters have been and continue to be well represented in the Specialty rings, and several can boast of multiple BISS wins (see Appendixes).

Ch. Windem's Lotsa Dots

            (photo from the author's collection)

By 1983, more English Setters arrived to reclaim the Best in Show ring. On the West Coast, Bob Wills' *Ch. Lorien's Fire Brigade*, initially shown by Bruce Schultz and later by Doug Johnson, had just begun his illustrious career. "Coalie" won *ESAA Dog of the Year* in *1983* and tied with Ch. Fantail's Sunshine Man for the *Rock Falls Colonel Award* for most BIS. Returning English Setters to the All-Breed level, Lorien's Fire Brigade continued to win Best in Shows and Specialties. During his half-decade career, "Coalie" carved his name among the top English of all time, winning *11 AKC BIS, 8 Specialty BISS*, and *ESAA's Rock Falls Colonel Award in 1986 and 1987*. He retired from active showing after winning the *1987 ESAA National Specialty*[5] from the Veterans class.

Ch. Lorien's Fire Brigade
(Rinehart photo from the author's collection)

A great Canadian dog, *Ch. Fantail's Sunshine Man*, owned by Frank and Carole Felice and bred by Honey Glendinning (an internationally licensed judge), claimed *1984* as his own by winning the *ESAA National Specialty* and *ESAA's Dog of the Year and Rock Falls Colonel Awards*. He retired in 1985 with *5 AKC BIS* in America[6] and went on to win more than *90 Canadian BIS*.

Ch. Fantail's Sunshine Man

(photo from the author's collection)

At the midpoint of the decade, still more English Setters were finding their way to the Best in Show ring. On the East Coast, Barbara Oak's ***Ch. Neverdone Five Oaks Victor,*** shown by Mark Threfell for Dot Berry, swept top honors in ***1985,*** winning the ***National Specialty, ESAA's Dog of the Year Award,*** and the ***Rock Falls Colonel Award*** with ***3 AKC BIS.*** Victor took ***3 BISS*** between 1985 and 1989.[7]

Ch. Neverdone Five Oaks Victor

(photo from the author's collection)

In 1986 *Ch. Wickett Buckhannon* (another Barrister Beau son), also shown by Mark Threfell for Dot Beery and breeder Mary Margaret Ruth, became the top Breed-level English by winning *ESAA Dog of the Year*, while *Ch. Stagedoor Star of Abbyroad*, a beautiful tri-color bitch bred by Joan Savage and owned by Mary Schmitt, won the *ESAA National Specialty*. Many other English were consistently winning at the Specialty, Group, and All-Breed levels. Among these wonderful Setters were two stunning blue Beltons: *Ch. Kelyric Blueprint*, bred, owned, and shown by Dennis and Karen Kennedy to *8 BISS and a BIS*; and Sara and Betty Sly's *Ch. Seal Rock's English Trifle with 3 BISS*. A pair of beautiful bitches also delighting the fancy were *Ch. Goodtime Glory Rosebud* (bred by Angie Sparkes and leased to Elsworth Howell) and the Braggs' *Ch. Wileire Holly Go Lightly*, each with *3 BISS* and multiple Group firsts. These two, along with Janice Knight's *Ch. Hemlock Lane-O'Lawdy's Time Out*, with *5 BISS*, were lighting up rings from coast to coast.[8]

Ch. Kelyric Blueprint
   (Fox & Cook photo courtesy of Dennis & Karen Kennedy- Kelyric)

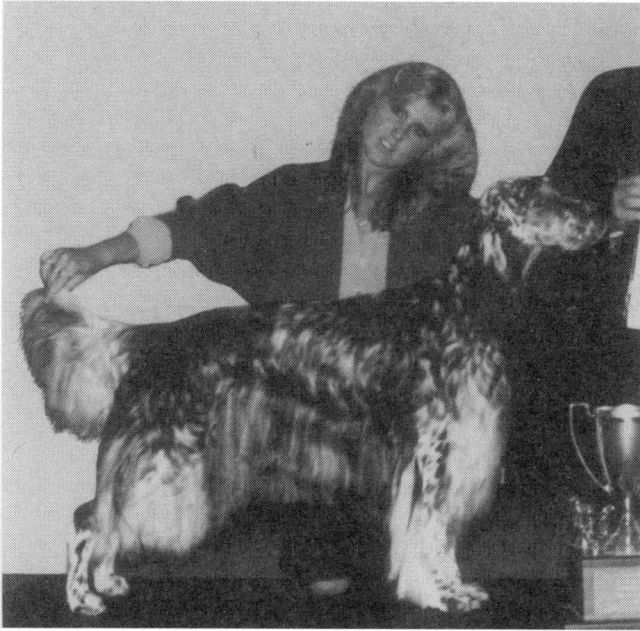

Ch. Stagedoor Star of Abbyroad
(photo from the author's collection)

Ch. Goodtime Glory Rosebud
(photo courtesy Craig & Angie Sparkes-Goodtime)

Ch. Wileire Holly Go Lightly
(photo courtesy of Garth Gourlay archives)

Moving into the last half of the decade, the English Setter fancy and the dog world witnessed the greatest trio since Ch. Rock Falls Colonel, his brother Racket, and Ch. Ludar of Blue Bar were shown in the early '50s. These three outstanding dogs would propel the breed back into national prominence.

In *1986*, even as a youngster, *Ch. Foxtract's The Invincible One*, bred by Dick Fox and shown in the East by Mark Threfell, had demonstrated his greatness by going *Best of Opposite Sex in the 1986 ESAA Futurity.* Then in 1987 "Vince" won *ESAA's Dog of the Year* and *Rock Falls Colonel Awards* (tied with Ch. Lorien's Fire Brigade). This was just the start of his rise to prominence. In *1988* he became the first English Setter since the Colonel to rise to national rankings at the All-Breed level, finishing 1988 as the No. 4 dog All-Breed with *13 BIS* and *50 Group firsts*, and winning *ESAA's Dog of the Year* and *Rock Falls Colonel Awards* for the second consecutive year. "Vince" retired in 1990 with an admirable record of *16 AKC BIS* and *6 BISS.*[9]

Ch. Foxtract's The Invincible One
(photo courtesy of Dick Fox – Foxtract)

The second dog of this trio was Bob and Peggy Dunsmuir's *Ch. Timbertrail's Riptide*, shown by Ken Murray in the Midwest. Riptide set an enviable pace between *1986 and 1990*, winning an impressive *14 AKC BIS* (the No. 9 all-time record for English Setters) and *9 BISS* in a career that spanned five years. Ch. Timbertrail's Riptide is the holder of the *record for English Setter Best of Breed wins with 285*.[10] In just a few years, Bob Dunsmuir had forged another link in the chain of great English Setters. With the Best in Show and Specialty performances of Billy, Coalie, Sunshine Man, Victor, Vince, and Riptide, English Setters were truly back in the high life.

In 1988 a two-year-old bitch from California was about to burst onto the scene. Goodtime Kennels, the kennels of my wife, Angie Sparkes, were typical of the small show/hobby kennels of the 1970s and 1980s. What was very different was that in 1975, while we were living in the Midwest, we had acquired a foundation bitch from Marge O'Connell's Hiddenlane line. After moving to California in 1977, Angie and her new partner, Judy Fassler, bred her foundation bitch (a granddaughter of Hiddenlane's Merry Max and Hiddenlane

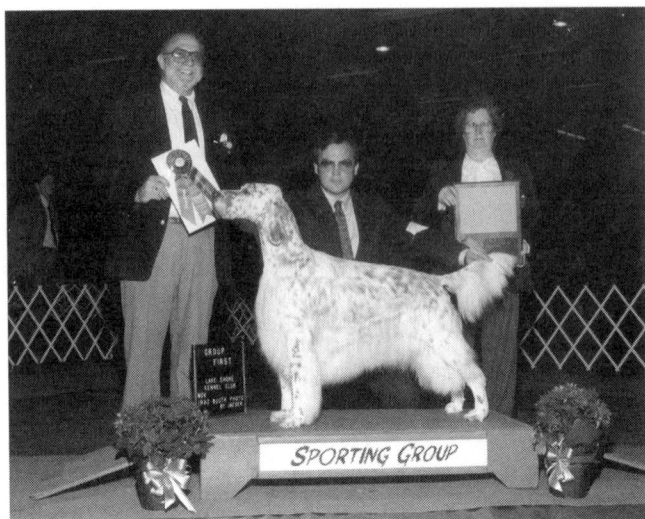

Ch. Timbertrail's Riptide
(photo courtesy of Bob & Peggy Dunsmuir-Timbertrail)

Blue Turquoise) and produced a litter with two exceptional bitches. One, Ch. Goodtime Glory Rosebud, was leased to Elsworth Howell and was the last English Setter he campaigned before his untimely death. In 1986 they bred Rosebud's litter sister to Neal Weinstein's Ch. Guys 'n Dolls Jericho Lark (a Shalimar Duke grandson owned by the Grimms), and this joining of the two great lines of the '70s (Hiddenlane and Guys 'n Dolls) produced a stunning bitch that would make English Setter history—Ch. Goodtime's Silk Teddy.

Ch. Goodtime's Silk Teddy (shown by Bruce Schultz) came on the scene in *1988*, winning her first *ESAA National Specialty* (only her twelfth show as a Special) and 2 All-Breed BIS. In 1989 the 3 greatest Setters of the decade, Vince, Riptide, and Silk Teddy, met for the only time together in the ring at the Westminster KC in what was one of the most electric breed rings ever at the Garden. Silk Teddy went on to glory that day, with Best of Breed and third in Group, and finished *1989* in spectacular fashion. She was the *No. 2 dog All Breed* with an incredible *22 BIS* and 81 Group firsts, the *Quaker Oats Sporting Dog of the Year Award* (the only other English Setter to do so was Rock Falls Colonel), her *second ESAA National Specialty*, and *virtually all top ESAA honors*. Silk Teddy closed out the decade in

1990 as she began, winning her record-tying *third National Specialty* and finishing the year as the *No. 9 dog All-Breed* with *15 BIS and 66 Group 1s*. This amazing English Setter bitch holds the *all-time English Setter record of 163 Group 1s*, breaking the record of the legendary Ch. Rock Falls Colonel. She is tied with the great Ch. Guys 'n Dolls Annie O'Brien with *three consecutive National Specialty wins* and is the *third-best English Setter in history in AKC Best in Show wins with 39*, behind Ch. Rock Falls Colonel's 100 and Ch. Maro of Maridor's 55. Shown mostly at All-Breed shows, she still won *11 BISS*.[11] One of her least known but most noteworthy achievements was that between June 1988 and her last two shows in January 1991, she was shown a total of 275 times and won Best of Breed 259 times. That means that like the great Rock Falls Colonel before her, Silk Teddy lost the Breed only sixteen times in her life! Silk Teddy had a zest for life and the show ring that was truly captivating. She obviously enjoyed herself, and we had a wonderful time just watching her. Bruce and Gretchen Schultz wrote a very moving piece about Silk Teddy (known to us as "Haley") for the *1997 ESAA Annual*, in which they said,

Ch. Goodtime's Silk Teddy
(Missy photo courtesy Craig & Angie Sparkes-Goodtime)

When showtime arrived, for Haley it was as if the party started! She celebrated each showday by taking her heart, her pizzazz, and magnetism into showring after show- ring. She truly had spirit and heart, in addition to being the ultimate "Lady Ambassador" for the English Setter Breed. She captured the hearts of competitors, spectators, and judges, but most importantly, ours!...Haley, dear friend, we feel blessed to have shared in your life and thank you for the happiness and memories you brought into ours.

After winning her record-breaking 163rd Group first, Bruce handed her lead to me and said, *"Take her home now, she has nothing left to prove!"* She was never shown again and lived to the age of twelve as the rightful queen of the house. I am thankful to have dozens of videocassette reels that record her career. They're almost as exciting to watch now as she was to watch then.

Ch. Goodtime's Silk Teddy—1989 ESAA National
(photo courtesy Craig & Angie Sparkes-Goodtime)

At the Del Valle KC show in early 1988 (at the time, one of the largest All-Breed shows in the country), Neal Weinstein knocked on the door of our motor home and summarily announced he was there to groom Silk Teddy. Just as Joe Kaziny did with the Trotters twenty-five years earlier, he spent hours teaching Angie the "California technique" that would typify Silk Teddy for her entire career. Later that day, as if to complete the reenactment, her co-owner/breeder, Judy Fassler, handled her before Bob Dunsmuir (breeder and owner of Ch. Timbertrail's Riptide), who awarded Haley the points to finish her and launch her Specials career.

Ch. Goodtime's Silk Teddy finishing photo with judge Robert Dunsmuir
(Fox & Cook photo courtesy Craig & Angie Sparkes-Goodtime)

These five best-winning English Setters of the decade (Billy, Coalie, Vince, Riptide, and Silk Teddy) accounted for an amazing 92 AKC BIS, 44 BISS, and 5 ESAA Nationals, an achievement that ranks them with the great English Setters of any previous decade.

Among the other English Setters who had wonderful show careers in the '80s and deserve recognition was *Ch. Mysti's Triumph of Valley Run* with *3 BISS between 1983 and 1985*. And Tom and Roberta Williams were in the high life with their *Ch. Willglen Major Motion*, who won *4 BISS between 1987 and 1989*, and a lovely bitch,

Ch. Willglen Liberty Celebration, with *6 BISS between 1988 and 1991.*[12]

One other remarkable event occurred during the '80s. In *1985 Dual Ch. Heathrow's Rainbow Robber*, owned by Peter and Mary Ann Samuelson, became the first English Setter in the history of the breed to earn championships in both show and field trials. "Alex" was an English Setter Specialty BISS winner as well, and began the resurgence of interest in hunting the bench type of English Setter. Today, thanks to the interest he generated, the English Setter Association of America has a Hunting Test, and there are now nearly a dozen Dual Champion English Setters.[13]

The decade of the '80s saw the return of English Setters to the top ranks of the dog show world. These beautiful animals now passed the torch to the Setters that would close out the millennium.

Endnotes

1. *AKC Gazettes*, 1977-81.

2. *AKC Gazettes*, 1979-84.

3. Ibid.

4. Ibid.

5. *AKC Gazettes*, 1982-87.

6. Ibid.

7. *AKC Gazette Award Issues*, 1984 and 1990.

8. Ibid.

9. Ibid.

10. Ibid.

11. *AKC Gazette Award Issues*, 1988-91.

12. *AKC Gazette Award Issues*, 1980-91.

13. M. A. Samuelson, "English Setter Dual Champions," *2001 ESAA Annual.*

Chapter Eight

The 1990s—Cruising in High Gear

1997 ESAA National Specialty Best of Breed judging
(photo from author's collection)

The decade of the '80s returned English Setters to national prominence in the Group and Best in Show rings. The winning begun by Billy, Coalie, and Sunshine Man was carried on by Vince, Riptide, and the incomparable Silk Teddy. English Setters were again a force to be reckoned with in the Group and Best in Show rings.

Ch. Goodtime's Silk Teddy began the *1990s* with her final year on the circuit. She won her *third consecutive ESAA National Specialty* and was the *No. 9 dog All Breed* at year's end with another *15 BIS and 61 Group firsts.* The English Setters that had competed against her in the final years of the '80s now had the ring to themselves. And they took good advantage. Top-winning Setters appeared in ESAA regions throughout the country.

Ch. Goodtime's Silk Teddy – 1990 ESAA National
(photo courtesy Craig & Angie Sparkes-Goodtime)

Ch. Kelyric California Sun, bred by Dennis and Karen Kennedy, owned by Dot Berry, Lise Trottier, and Louis Journalt of Canada and campaigned by Mark Threfell, was ***ESAA Dog of the Year in 1991*** and came out of retirement to win the ***ESAA National in 1994*** (owner handled by Lise Trottier). In his career, "Calif" won a total of ***10 BISS***.[2]

In ***1991*** the ***Rock Falls Colonel Award*** went to Pam LeFever and Joe Kicska's ***Ch. Brasswinds Sitn' ona Gold Mine***. "Bobby," shown by Laurel Leonard, had a long and rewarding career, winning ***ESAA Dog of the Year*** and his ***second Rock Falls Colonel Award in 1992***. When Bobby retired in 1993, he had won ***5 AKC BIS and 10 BISS***,[3] and remains the third-highest Best of Breed winner with 269 ribbons. Pam LeFever followed up Bobby's success with a lovely bitch, ***Ch. Brasswinds Cinnamon Sugar***. "Sugar" won a very creditable ***5 BISS*** in her career between 1993 and 1995, including the Combined Setter Specialty in 1995.[4]

Ch. Esquires Blizzard of Carob, a beautiful orange bitch bred by Carol Ulrich, won the ***ESAA National Specialty in 1991***. Shown by

Ch. Kelyric California Sun
  (photo courtesy of Lise Trottier and Louis Journalt — Artizoe)

her owner Suzy Kerwin, she was the first recipient of the Goodtime Challenge Trophy, donated by Goodtime Kennels upon retirement of the Rock Falls Racket Challenge Trophy and presented to the winner of the ESAA National Specialty. The following year, 1992, with the National back in California, Washington state's *Ch. Ash Hollows Why Stop Now*, shown by his breeder-owner Kevin Chestnut, became the first dog from this region to win the *ESAA National*. "Sam," who won *3 AKC BIS*, was a stunning orange Belton with a lovely sprinkling of orange flecks over a pure white coat. He was one of the most visually pleasing English Setters in a long while.[5]

Keeping the ESAA National title in Washington state was Melissa Newman's *Dual Ch. Set'r Ridge's Solid Gold*. "Hadji" is the all-time top producer in English Setters with more than 120 championship get. He is the epitome of what an English Setter can be in that he was a top show dog (*4 AKC BIS* and *10 BISS* in his career[6]) and went on to earn his Dual championship in the field after he retired from the ring. Solid Gold was the winner of the *1988 ESAA Futurity*, an Award of Merit in 1988, and BOS in the 1989, 1991, and 1998

Ch. Esquires Blizzard of Carob
                    (photo from the author's collection)

Ch. Ash Hollows Why Stop Now
                    (photo from the author's collection)

ESAA Nationals—the lattermost from the Field Trial Class when he was twelve years old. Hadji's win at the *1993 ESAA National* was a very popular one indeed. He was a strong presence at Nationals and any Specialty he attended. Hadji's sister, *Ch. Set'r Ridge's Blueprint Zabri*, was a *BIS* and multiple Specialty winner as well. Zabri and Hadji were the second brother and sister pair (though not litter mates) to win BISS and BOS at the same National, accomplishing the feat in 1993; Zabri finished her career with *3 BISS*.[7]

Dual Ch. Set'r Ridge's Solid Gold
    (Callea photo courtesy of Melissa Newman – Set'r Ridge)

Ch. Set'r Ridge's Blueprint Zabri
    (Fox & Cook photo courtesy of Garth Gourlay archives)

In 1992 another of Angie Sparkes' Goodtime Setters, *Ch. Good-time Royale Salute* (a Shalimar Duke great-grandson), began his Specials career. Handled by Bradley Buttner, a former top Junior Showman turned professional, Royal Salute quickly rose to prominence, being named *ESAA Dog of the Year in 1993*, his second year on the circuit. He retired from active showing in 1994 but was taken to Specialties until he was eight. By the end of 1997 he had won an impressive *10 BISS* (No. 10 for English Setters all time) and was BOS at the 1997 ESAA National at eight years of age.[8]

Ch. Goodtime Royale Salute
   (Fox & Cook photo courtesy Craig & Angie Sparkes-Goodtime)

While Royale Salute was winning top honors at the Breed and Specialty level, another of Bob and Peggy Dunsmuir's Timbertrail dogs was adding his name to the list of great English Setters. *Ch. Timbertrail's Sign of Trent*, a Riptide son shown by Ken Murray, was *ESAA Dog of the Year in 1994* and *Rock Falls Colonel winner in 1993 and 1994*. In his show career between 1992 and 1996, "Trent" won *6 AKC BIS* and *7 BISS*.[9]

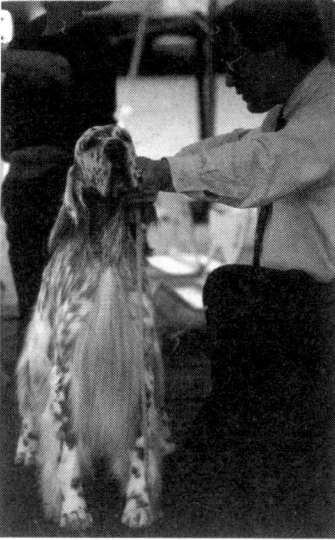

Ch. Timbertrail's Sign of Trent
(photo courtesy of Garth Gourlay archives)

The mid-'90s saw another of Carol Ulrich's Carob setters, *Ch. Carob Painted on Jeans* (a son of Foxtract's The Invincible One), achieve success. Painted on Jeans was the winner of the *1992 ESAA Futurity* (just as his sire, Vince, was a winner in 1986) and followed up this promising start by winning the *1995 ESAA National Specialty* and a total of *3 BISS* in his career.[10]

Ch. Carob Painted on Jeans
(photo from the author's collection)

Meanwhile, back in California, *Ch. Set'r Ridge's Lookin' at You Kid*, shown by Taffy McFadden for Melissa Newman and J. Decker, was a very consistent BIS winner. Kid was *ESAA's Rock Falls Colonel Award winner in 1994, 1995, and 1996*, and finished his career with an admirable *13 AKC BIS* and *5 BISS*.[11]

Ch. Set'r Ridge's Lookin' at You Kid
(photo from the author's collection)

Ch. Country Squire Lone Star from Colorado had a wonderful career keeping English Setters well represented in the mountain states. Shown by his breeder-owner, Shaun Jordon, Squire won *6 AKC BIS* and *3 BISS* in his career between 1996 and 1999. He was *ESAA's Rock Falls Colonel Award winner in 1997 and 1998*.[12]

Bitches were strong at the end of the decade, with daughters of Solid Gold becoming a force at the National and Regional Specialty levels. In 1996 a lovely and spirited Specials bitch, in the tradition of Silk Teddy, sparkled in the Breed, Group, and Best in Show rings. *Ch. Lampliter's Attah-Tud O'Trabeiz* (a Solid Gold daughter), owned by Drs. Foster and Smith and Peg Ziebart and shown by professional handler Carlos Puig, was the *1995, 1996, and 1997 ESAA Dog of the Year*. "Tuddy" was the winner of *back-to-back ESAA National Specialties in 1996 and 1997*. She finished her career with *4 AKC BIS, 8 BISS*, and a BOS (from the Veterans Class) at the 2001 ESAA National.[13]

Ch. Lampliter's Attah-Tud O'Trabeiz
(photo from the author's collection)

Another Solid Gold daughter who made her presence at Nationals was **Ch. Reidwood Poetry in Motion**, owned by Nancy Warner and the Reids. She went BOS in 1994 and took Award Of Merit (AOM) in 1995, 1996, and 1997 before winning the whole thing at the *1998 ESAA Nationals* (and at this National, her daughter Ch. Reidwood Symphony in Motion went Best in Futurity). A *BIS* winner, this simply beautiful orange Belton bitch was formidable in the regional specialty ring, winning a total of *14 Specialty BISS*, the record for English Setter bitches that stood until 2002.[14] She closed her wonderful career by winning another AOM at the 1999 National.

The 1999 National was witness to another English Setter "first." *Ch. Trabeiz Premonition of a Dream*, an Atta-Tud daughter, won the 1999 ESAA National Specialty. While sons and daughters of male National winners have won the National, "Chiquita" and her dam, "Tuddy," are the first and as yet only mother and daughter to have both won the National. After her Nationals win, Chiquita retired from the ring with a *BIS* and an admirable total of *7 Specialty BISS* in her career.[15]

*Ch. Reidwood Poetry in Motion
(photo courtesy of Nancy Warner)*

At the *1998 National,* the fancy saw a stunningly handsome light orange male, ***Ch. Honeygait Goodtime Hot Topic,*** win BOS in the ***ESAA Futurity.*** "Travis," owned by Angie Sparkes of Goodtime Kennels, did not take long to justify his Futurity win; he finished his championship by taking Winners Dog at the National Specialty the very next day. In her description of the Futurity in the *1998 ESAA Annual,* Jane Wooding, ESAA Futurity Chair, said,

> *Our Futurity continues to be an indicator of the quality in our breed. Many of the winners go on to be our biggest winners and best producers. We didn't have to wait long this year to see an example of this as our BOS in Futurity* [Hot Topic] *went on later in the week to be chosen Winners Dog.*

Hot Topic had a short but memorable Specials career, winning ***ESAA's Dog of the Year*** and ***Rock Falls Colonel Awards in 1999.*** In only eighteen months Travis took *4 AKC BIS* and *7 Specialty BISS,*[16] including a BOS at the 1999 ESAA National, as well as an Award of Merit at the 2000 National. Appropriately for the scheme of this book, ***Travis won the last Sporting Group of the millennium in December 1999.***

Ch. Honeygait Goodtime Hot Topic
   (Fox & Cook photo courtesy Craig & Angie Sparkes-Goodtime)

Ch. Honeygait Goodtime Hot Topic w/ Ken Murray
   (photo courtesy Craig & Angie Sparkes-Goodtime)

Yes, as the decade of the 1990s and the millennium ended, English Setters were cruising in high gear. The "winning strain" was still capable of rising to the occasion and creating a wonderful Setter that could light up the show ring. English Setters were and are winning Best in Shows and Sporting Groups as we move into the next millennium. The kennels of Fieldplay, Foxtract, Goodtime, Set'r Ridge, Brasswinds, and Carob kept faith with the breeders of the past. C. N. Myers, A. A. Mitten, J. J. Sinclair, Davis Tuck, and Bill Holt would be pleased to see the breed in such good hands.

Endnotes

1.   *Science Diet, Inc.*, Annual Awards–1990.

2.   *AKC Gazette Award Issues*, 1990-2000.

3.   Ibid.

4.   Ibid.

5.   Ibid.

6.   Ibid.

7.   Ibid.

8.   Ibid.

9.   Ibid.

10.   Ibid.

11.   Ibid.

12.   Ibid.

13.   Ibid.

14.   Ibid.

15.   Ibid.

16.   Ibid.

Chapter Nine

The First Decade of the Next Millennium

Records Are Made to Be Broken

As of the date of publication, only three years are available for review. Yet in those three years, English Setters continue to make their presence felt in the Specialty, Group, and Best in Show rings as their predecessors did in the decades past. And as in the past, more English reached national heights.

The millennium began on the ESAA National Specialty scene with Pam LeFever's ***Ch. Brasswinds Sunrise Ahhmen*** winning the ***2000 National*** and living up to the promise he had shown as the winner of the ***1999 Futurity***. Brasswinds continues to produce top winning English Setters.

Ch. Oakley's Cigar, a blue Belton from Washington state, owned by Jim and Bobbie Janard and Paula Dempsey, won the ***2001 ESAA National***. Cigar had great success in his Specials career, winning ***5 AKC BIS, ESAA's Rock Falls Colonel Award in 2000***, and a total of ***7 BISS*** before retiring after his Nationals win.[1]

The new millennium was also witness to two stunning bitches that dominated the show rings in a fashion similar to Vince, Riptide, and Silk Teddy in the late 1980s. The first of these, ***Ch. Set'r Ridges Wyndswept in Gold***, a lovely orange Belton bitch, owned by Dr. and Mrs. William Truesdale[2] and shown admirably by Kellie Fitzgerald,[3]

Ch. Oakley's Cigar

(photo courtesy of Paula Dempsey - Oakley)

had a fantastic show career in which she won an impressive *14 AKC BIS* and a record-breaking *18 Specialty BISS.*[4] "Bria" had an incredible run in *2002* and was the *No. 1 Sporting Dog* in the country as well as *No. 1 English Setter* (all systems). This is an accomplishment not achieved since Ch. Goodtime's Silk Teddy won the Quaker Oats Award in 1989. Bria was also the *No. 6 dog All-Breed in 2002*, joining a very select list of English Setters to ever rank in the top ten at the All-Breed level.[5] Bria broke the record for bitches previously held by Ch. Reidwoods Poetry in Motion and is now the *top Specialty-winning English Setter bitch.* She crowned her Specialty record by winning the *2002 ESAA National.*

Another beautiful bitch, *Ch. Honeygait N Lampliter Fever* (Hot Topic's litter sister), bred by John and Mary Nowak and shown by Ken Murray for her owners, Dave and Judy Mates and John and Mary Nowak, was ruling the show rings in the heartland of America. Fever was *ESAA's English Setter of the Year in 2000, 2001, and 2002* and the *ESAA Rock Falls Colonel Award winner in 2001 and 2002.* During that time she continued the dominance of English Setters in

Ch. Set'r Ridges Wyndswept in Gold
(photo courtesy of Debra Mack & Elliott Weiss - Wyndswept)

the Group and Best in Show rings by winning an awe inspiring *38 AKC BIS* (fourth best in English Setter history) as well as *13 BISS* (also fourth best in English Setter history), and **270 Best of Breed wins (a record for English Setter bitches)** thus far in her career.[6] Fever was the *No. 3 Sporting Dog in both 2001 and 2002* and won the *Nature's Recipe Sporting Group Award in 2002*. This was the first time an English Setter had won this award since Ch. Goodtime's Silk Teddy accomplished the feat in 1989. Fever also had the distinction in 2001of winning the last ESAA Combined Setter Specialty, a show that has now been replaced with other pre-Garden Specialties.

Other English Setters that have achieved success early in this decade include two more beautiful bitches. *Ch. Fieldplay's Windy Skye*, bred and owned by Bob and Frances Stevens and Dot Berry and handled by Susan Allen, has *8 BISS* in her career to date.[7] *Ch. Reidwood Symphony in Motion*, the *1998 ESAA Futurity winner*, owned by D. Black, B. Gideon, Nancy Warner, and C. Reid, lived up to expectations with *4 Specialty BISS* in her brief career.[8]

Ch. Honeygait N Lampliter Fever
    (Downey photo courtesy of David & Judy Mates - Lampliter)

English Setter males have also been active on the Specialty scene, with ***Ch. Trabeiz Premier Element of Surprise***, an ***AKC BIS*** winner owned by Drs. Foster and Smith and Peg Ziebart and shown by Carlos Puig, adding ***5 BISS*** ribbons to his collection; and Jill Warren's ***Ch. Esthetes Splendor in the Grass***, another winning blue Belton, has picked up ***6 BISS*** thus far.[9]

Other young males of note are: ***Ch. Brooklin Driftwood Dreamquest***, owned by Linda Mackenzie; ***Ch. Sunshine Palace S. Golden State*** (a Solid Gold son), owned by Sumiko Ikeda; ***Ch. Indian Bend Hot Item of Pamir*** (a Hot Topic son), bred by Sandi McCue and owned by Don and Georgean Jensen; and Nancy Warner and Iris Reid's ***Ch. Reidwood Artistry in Motion*** all demonstrated that the males could hold their own at Specialties with ***3 BISS*** apiece.[10]

With the quality of English Setters across the county and the increased numbers of shows and Specialties, good Setters have every opportunity to join the list of record holders.

Many of the finest judges and professional handlers in AKC are closely identified with English Setters; the next chapter will discuss this relationship in detail.

Ch. Esthetes Splendor in the Grass
   (Rinehart photo courtesy of Jill Warren – Esthete's)

Endnotes

1. *AKC Gazette Award Issues*, 1999-2002.

2. Ch. Set'r Ridge Wyndswept in Gold was originally owned by Debra Mack and Elliott Weiss. She was being campaigned by Dorthea (Dot) Berry. Dot Berry (Of B Kennels) was a revered member of the English Setter Association of America since 1947 and has owned and campaigned some of the greatest English Setters in history. Her best-known English was Ch. Foxtract The Invincible One (see Chapter 7). Dot Berry passed away in mid-2002, and Dr. and Mrs. William Truesdale (HiTech Kennels), a remarkable couple who are most widely known for their top winning boxers, acquired and guided Bria in her incredible year and finished what Dot Berry began.

3. Kellie Fitzgerald is a top professional handler in the sporting breeds. She has already won Best in Show at Westminster Kennel Club in 2000 with the famous Springer Spaniel Ch. Salilyn N Erin's Shameless, owned by the late Julia Gasow. She also managed Julia's kennel for many years.

4. *AKC Gazette Award Issues*, 1999-2002.

5. This very select list includes Ch. Blue Dan of Happy Valley, Ch. Maro of Maridor, Ch. Rock Falls Colonel, Ch. Foxtract The Invincible One, and Ch. Goodtime's Silk Teddy.

6. *AKC Gazette Award Issues*, 1999-2002. In early 2003, after this book went to publication, Fever has won her 40th Best in Show to become the Top Best in Show winning English Setter bitch. The author congratulates her and thanks the publisher for the ability to insert this note.

7. Susan Allen is an up-and-coming Canadian handler. She is the daughter of Norma Allen (Milroy Kennels) and has been winning Specialties and Groups on many English Setters in the United States and Canada.

8. *AKC Gazette Award Issues*, 1999-2002.

9. Ibid.

10. Ibid.

Chapter Ten

Handlers, Judges, and English Setters

"Fun with Dick & Jane"- Jane (Kamp) Forsyth (with Ch. Storybooks Best Seller) and Dick Cooper (with Ch. Seasac Knight of Canterbury) at the 1978 ESAA National Specialty

Both extensive research and long experience indicate that two "rules" must be followed to achieve success in the show ring. They are fairly simple:

■ 1. Start with a great dog.
■ 2. Have a talented handler or owner show the dog.

An English Setter—or Gordon or Irish or other long-coated breed—requires conditioning, grooming, and presentation that are specialized to the breed. Many of the best-known professional

105

handlers (and those who have gone on to become well-known judges) have had a special affinity and identification with English Setters. This chapter pays homage to some of the special people who have contributed to the success of a number of the greatest English Setters mentioned in this book. We focus on professional handlers in this chapter, as the owner-handlers have been well chronicled.

We start with the handler widely acknowledged to be the best of all, ***Benjamin F. Lewis, Jr.*** Benny Lewis handled many sporting dogs but is best known for his prowess with the dogs of Dr. A. A. Mitten's Happy Valley Kennels in the 1930s. In the English Setter section of the AKC's 1968 edition of *The Complete Dog Book,* the following appeared:

> *The first show for English setters was held at Newcastle-on-Tyne on January 28, 1859, and from this time on dog shows flourished throughout England, gradually increasing in popularity. English Setters became increasingly popular, and it is of interest in passing to note that in 1930 for the first time an American was invited abroad to judge English Setters. The expert so honored was none other than the late Benjamin F. Lewis Jr. of Lansdowne, PA, who has been associated with English Setters since his boyhood. His father, B. F. Lewis, born in South Wales, for many years was unquestionably the outstanding handler of all sporting show dogs in America and it is believed that no one will dissent from the opinion that his son, the late Benny, was without an equal as a handler of sporting dogs.*

Benny was on the lead of such great Happy Valley dogs as ***Ch. Blue Dan of Happy Valley***, ***Ch. The Country Gentleman***, and ***Ch. Pilot of Crombie of Happy Valley***. In a recent interview, Marsha Hall Brown recalled that judges and handlers of the late 1940s and '50s who remembered Benny Lewis regarded him as without equal. Enos Phillips, Alec Pelan, Anthony Miller, and Dr. Milbank talked of Benny's peerless ability.[1]

Charles Palmer with Ch. Sturdy Max at Morris & Essex
(photo courtesy of St. Hubert's Animal Welfare Center, Madison N.J.)

A contemporary of Benny Lewis was the incomparable **Charles Palmer.** Charlie Palmer was the handler and kennel manager for Maridor Kennels and, after their dispersal sale in 1938, for Mrs. Priscilla Ryan's Prune's Own Kennels. He owned and handled **Ch. Lakelands Yuba, Ch. Sturdy Max,** and **Ch. Maro of Maridor** (later selling these dogs to Prune's Own Kennels). Charlie also owned Ch. Dora of Maridor (a litter sister to the great Maridor brothers) and bred her to Ch. Lakelands Yuba to produce Ch. Sturdy Max 2nd, a name found in the pedigrees of many of the English of the '40s and '50s. In a recent interview, Virginia Tuck Hall recalled Charlie Palmer as the "top handler of his day" with a "wonderful pair of hands."[2] Davis Tuck lists Charlie Palmer as one of the influential people credited with "bringing the modern English Setter, Laverack type, to its present state of excellence."[3]

As we move into the 1940s, C. N. Myers' Blue Bar Kennels became the dominant force in English Setters, and two handlers are renowned for their association with his dogs. The first was **Charles Davis,** who served Blue Bar from 1936 until 1943. Charlie Davis handled C. N.'s first Special, Ch. Smile of Stagboro, and was best known for his work with ***Ch. Lem of Blue Bar***, the National Specialty winner in 1943. During the heyday of his kennels, C. N. Myers used to ship his dogs to the shows by rail car. A famous story recounts a trip to New York on which Charlie and the dogs were accompanied by an orchestra to entertain the Myerses.[4] Charlie Davis was one of the professional handlers who saw Ch. Sturdy Max practicing in the benching area at the 1937 Morris & Essex. One can imagine his reaction to the consensus that another dog would win.[5]

After Charlie Davis retired in 1944, C. N. Myers hired ***Harold Correll***, who remained the main Blue Bar handler and kennel manager until Myers' death in 1953. An extremely talented man, he became an all-breed handler after his association with Blue Bar. He was the very first to be licensed by the newly formed Professional Handlers Association (PHA) and held PHA License #1.[6] Among the English Setters he handled were ***Ch. Rip of Blue Bar***, who won the Quaker Oats Award for the most Group firsts in the Eastern Region in 1948. Anne Rogers Clarke believed that Harold, and later his son, had a special affinity for English as well as Irish and Gordon Setters. She noted that he always had a Setter in the Group ribbons.[7] Jane Forsyth recalled an amusing show trait of Harold Correll. She said that when stacking and presenting the dog, he would place the ear on the show side of his English Setters "inside out"—that is, he would raise the earflap so the judge could look down the ear canal. While no one ever knew why he did this, Jane recalls that whenever she and Anne were in the ring with Harold, they would *all* show the ear "inside out."[8]

The early 1950s saw the demise of the large breeding kennels of Happy Valley, Silvermine, Maridor, and Blue Bar, and the rise of all-breed professional handlers who worked for a variety of owners. ***Jane Kamp*** (Forsyth) was one of the first of the great all-breed handlers. While she handled for many many clients in her career, she is best known for her work with the Sporting dogs of Mrs. Cheever Porter of New York City. Jane won her first *Gaines Handler of the Year Award* in 1963. In all of the interviews I have conducted with professional handlers and English Setter luminaries, Jane Kamp (Forsyth) is acknowledged as the greatest all-breed handler ever. Corky Vroom (himself one of the great all-breed handlers) said that Jane had "the

Harold Correll with Ch. Rip of Blue Bar
(photo from archives of Bill and Lovey Trotter- Flecka's)

greatest hands" of any handler he has ever seen. Virginia Tuck
Nichols Hall recalls that in the late 1940s a well-known AKC judge
named Anton Ross told Davis and Virginia Tuck of a talented young
woman and urged them to hire Jane for Silvermine Kennels. While
that did not occur, Virginia Tuck, Jane Kamp, and Anne Rogers
(Clark) became fast friends and traveled together to many shows in
the 1950s.[9] Jane handled many English Setters but is best known for
her success at ESAA National Specialties. She handled the National
Specialty winner at five different ESAA Nationals: ***Ch. Rock Falls
Racket*** (1954), ***Ch. Ike of Blue Bar*** (1955 and 1956), ***Ch. Candlewood Distinction*** (1963), and ***Ch. Storybooks Best Seller*** (1978). As
was mentioned in Chapter 5, Ch. Candlewood Distinction was her
biggest-winning English Setter in a career that began sixty-four years
ago. As a well-respected all-round AKC judge, she has won and
judged Best in Show at Westminster and was the breed judge at the
1984 ESAA National Specialty.

Jane Kamp with Ch. Rock Falls Racket
(photo courtesy of Garth Gourlay archives)

Her husband of thirty-seven years and fellow handler for fifteen years before that is *Robert Forsyth*, the son of a handler who began his own career in the 1940s. He knew many of the top handlers of the day, including Charlie Palmer, Charlie Davis, Art Mulvilhill, and Horace Hollands. Bob handled the great *Ch. Zamitz Jumping Jack* to his National Specialty and Best in Show wins and was the handler for the Valley Run Kennels of Rachael Van Buren. He was on the lead of *Ch. Stan the Man of Valley Run* and the beautiful tri-color bitch *Ch. Valley Run Dinah-mite*.

Bob and Jane Forsyth have been instrumental in the development of many top all-breed handlers. George Alston, Bobby Fisher, and Mark Threfell apprenticed under them, and many more handlers were tutored in their craft by the Forsyths. They have *both* won Best in Show at Westminster (he with a Whippet and she with a Boxer); they retired from handling together at the 1981 Westminster KC show, and both continue to have distinguished judging careers.[10]

Bob Forsyth with Ch. Valley Run Dinah Mite
(photo from archives of Gus Polley – Skidby)

In the Midwest, two famous handlers were closely associated with English Setters, primarily through Marge O'Connell. *Hayden ("Doc") Martin*, who later became a well-respected AKC judge, handled many of the Ben-Dar Setters for Marge and Bill Sears. Doc Martin is most closely associated with *Ch. Ben-Dar's Winning Stride*, whom he took over just a few months prior to the 1958 International KC in Chicago. Doc Martin went Best in Show that day and stayed on Stride thereafter.[11] As Marge's kennels evolved into Hiddenlane, she began a long association with *Horace Hollands*. Horace was the handler for *Ch. Ludar of Blue Bar* and many of the well-known Hiddenlane Setters, including *Ch. Hiddenlane's Merry Max* and *Ch. Hiddenlanes Bloomfield Babu*. Horace's daughter Carol would often take the lead from her father on these dogs. He clearly passed his skills on to her.[12] Carol is currently an AKC Rep.

Other talented and well-respected Setter handlers emerged in the Midwest. Among them was *Richard Cooper* from Chicago. Dick was a skilled Setter handler (both English and Irish) whose first big-winning English was *Ch. Margand Lord Baltimore* in the early

Hayden ("Doc") Martin with Ch. Ben-Dar's Winning Stride
(photo from archives of Bill and Lovey Trotter- Flecka's)

Horace Hollands with Ch. Ludar of Blue Bar
(photo from archives of Marsha Hall Brown)

1960s. He continued handling for another thirty years and was widely considered one of the most skilled Setter groomers. His dogs were impeccably put down, and no one in the Midwest could compare to his artistic grooming skills. Dick Cooper handled English Setters for Chuck Prieb in the mid-1970s (***Ch. Storybooks Best Seller*** and later ***Ch. Seasac Knight of Canterbury***) and was part of one of the most amusing events in English Setter "handler lore." Chuck had entered both his specials at the 1978 ESAA National Specialty, with Jane Forsyth handling Best Seller (to his Nationals win that year) and Dick handling Knight of Canterbury. Unknown to either handler, Chuck had also entered these two dogs in the Brace class, and after the regular classes finished, he asked the two handlers to show his dogs in that ring. Their winning photo was titled "Fun with Dick and Jane" and is a classic shot in the 1978 ESAA Annual.

Dick Cooper with Ch. Margand Lord Baltimore
(photo from archives of Bill and Lovey Trotter- Flecka's)

One of the finest professional handlers in his era was **William Trainor**, who lived in Massachusetts. He was a highly popular and enthusiastic handler who became a longtime president of the PHA. Bill Trainor was a masterful professional who handled *four* ESAA National winners: *Ch. Merry Rover of Valley Run* (1966), *Ch. Sir Kip of Manitou* (1968 and 1969), and *Ch. Drummont's Tasty's Billy* (1981), the last English Setter to go first in Group at Westminster. In addition to these Nationals winners, Bill Trainor was on the leads of *Ch. Highland's Whip of Penmaen* and *Ch. Guys 'n Dolls Taste of Honey*. Jane Forsyth, who sold Bill Trainor their kennel and taught Bill to groom both English and Irish Setters, recalled the first Irish Setter that Bill Trainor showed to her. She gently reminded him that Irish Setters are *not* groomed like English Setters and quickly scheduled another grooming clinic. Bill Trainor learned these early lessons well and was considered one of the finest groomers of show dogs in his time. His skills in the conditioning and care of show dogs were admired by all.[13]

Out in California, **Richard Webb** had already made a name for himself as a breeder of Best in Show Irish Setters with his Webbline Kennels. Jane Forsyth purchased one of his Irish for her client Mrs.

Bill Trainor with Ch. Sir Kip of Manitou
(photo from archives of Marsha Hall Brown)

Cheever Porter.[14] A very stylish performer, Dick Webb was the first handler for Neal Weinstein and showed Neal's two foundation males, *Ch. Guys 'n Dolls Shalimar Duke* (ESAA National Specialty winner in 1970) and Duke's son *Ch. Guys 'n Dolls Onassis*.

Weinstein's second handler was *Corky Vroom*. Corky apprenticed under the great all-breed handler Harry Sangster (breeder of Spaniels and Pointers) in the late 1950s and early 1960s; he was first licensed in 1966, and along with Mike Shea received the last all-breed handler licenses issued by the AKC.[15] Corky was the first professional handler of the great *Ch. Guys 'n Dolls Annie O'Brien* and won the 1974 Combined Setter Specialty and a BIS with her. He handled Linda Hunt Sullivan's *Ch. Charlin Rudolph* and the author's *Ch. Goodtime Royale Salute* among many English Setters on the West Coast. Corky Vroom is the current president of PHA and on the Advisory Board for the AKC Handler Registration. I am pleased to call Corky Vroom my friend and for many years have proudly displayed in my motor home a framed $100 bill I won from him on a football wager. No matter how much in handling fees I ever paid to Corky, we both knew who was ahead.

Corky Vroom with Ch. Guys 'n Dolls Annie O'Brien
(photo from archives of Gus Polley – Skidby)

Also closely associated with the English Setters of Neal Weinstein is *Raymond McGinnis*, who apprenticed under all-breed handler Mac McDonald (a Cocker Spaniel breeder) and was one of the most successful all-breed handlers on the West Coast during the 1970s and '80s. In the world of English Setters, he was best known as the handler of *Ch. Guys 'n Dolls Annie O'Brien* during her best year, 1975. Ray also piloted *Ch. Guys 'n Dolls Wild William* and *Ch. Guys 'n Dolls Candy Kisses* in their successful careers. In addition, he was on the lead of *Ch. Editions by Invitation Only*, a Best in Show and Multiple BISS-winning English Setter in the late 1980s. Once again, Bob and Jane Forsyth played an early role in this handler's life. They needed a skilled handler to handle the overflow dogs in their string at Westminster in the late 1960s (at that time Westminster was an all-breed dog show with non-champion classes as well as Specials). In recognition of Ray's obvious talents and his rising stature, they asked him to show some of their dogs. Jane said that for several years Ray would show between fifteen and twenty dogs for the Forsyths at the Garden. He often remarked about how much he learned from

Ray McGinnis with Ch. Guys 'n Dolls Wild William
(photo courtesy of Garth Gourlay archives)

handling for Bob and Jane Forsyth at Westminster.[16] Ray McGinnis must be looked at as one of the modern master handlers. He and his wife, Jeanette, are now very popular AKC judges, and English Setter owners are proud to show before them.

As the 1970s closed, three men in three different areas of the country were establishing themselves as top sporting dog handlers. In California, *Bruce Schultz*, originally from Minnesota and later Arizona, began as a breeder of English Setters under the Rimrock Setter name. He apprenticed under Patty Grant and showed Yvonne Ward's *Ch. Sunburst Special Edition* to the 1977 ESAA Nationals win, as well as piloting *Ch. Lorien's Fire Brigade* for Bob Willis. Bruce married Gretchen Schallenbarger, daughter of Walt and Jo Schallenbarger of Gretchenhof German Shorthair Pointer fame (successful professional handlers as well). Together Bruce and Gretchen made a dynamic duo in the ring. They also showed my *Ch. Goodtime Glory Rosebud* prior to her lease by Elsworth Howell, but Bruce is best known in the English Setter world for the incredible campaign of

Bruce Shultz with Ch. Goodtime's Silk Teddy (photo courtesy Craig & Angie Sparkes-Goodtime)

Ch. Goodtime's Silk Teddy. Adding her three ESAA National wins to his 1977 victory, he ties Bill Trainor with *four* wins each, second only to Jane Forsyth's five ESAA National wins. Today, Bruce and Gretchen remain two of the top all-breed handlers on the West Coast.

On the East Coast, *Mark Threfell* made his presence felt. Mark also apprenticed under Bob and Jane Forsyth, and he too learned well. He won the 1985 ESAA National Specialty with *Ch. Neverdone Five Oaks Victor* and had No. 1-ranked English Setters with *Ch. Wickett Buckhannon* and *Ch. Kelyric California Sun*. His most memorable English was *Ch. Foxtract's The Invincible One*. Mark was a very active and energetic handler and a past president of PHA. Retired from handling, he is now associated with the Animal Planet network. Jane Forsyth recalls how she trained Mark (and George Alston) in grooming techniques. She would groom only the show side of her dogs and have Mark and George finish the dog's other side. According to her, they spent many hours attempting to master her techniques.[17]

Mark Threfell with Ch. Foxtract's The Invincible One
(photo from author's collection)

In the Midwest, *Ken Murray*, originally from Texas, had a long and fruitful apprenticeship under the great Dick Cooper. While Ken has had a number of top-winning dogs, he is best known for his success with Setters. Ken has shown Best in Show English, Irish, and Gordon Setters. He has mastered the grooming skills taught to him by Dick Cooper, and his Setters are always beautifully put down. Ken's first big-winning English was Bob and Peggy Dunsmuir's *Ch. Timbertrail's Riptide*, and he followed that campaign with their *Ch. Timbertrail's Sign of Trent* in 1994. His two most recent big winners were the author's 1999 English Setter of the Year, Ch. Honeygait Goodtime Hot Topic, and his litter sister *Ch. Honeygait N Lampliter Fever*, owned by Dave and Judy Mates and breeders John and Mary Nowak.

Ken Murray with Ch. Honeygait N Lampliter Fever
(photo courtesy of David & Judy Mates - Lampliter)

As mentioned earlier in this book, Bruce Schultz, Mark Threfell, and Ken Murray found themselves rivals in the memorable breed competition at the 1989 Westminster show. With each of these successful English Setter handlers showing his best English in a truly riveting contest, it was a thrill to watch the "best of the best" (both handlers and Setters) compete that day.

As this book goes to press, there are other English Setter handlers staking claims to greatness. *Carlos Puig* showed *Ch. Lampliter's Attah-Tud O' Trabeiz* to ESAA Nationals wins in 1996 and 1997 and followed that success with another No. 1 English Setter in 1998, *Ch. Sevenoaks Golden Garters.* Carlos is a top all-breed handler who, like those before him, seems to have an affinity for English Setters.

In Canada, *Will Alexander* has had remarkable success breaking all the Canadian Kennel Club English Setter records with Lise Trottier's and Lois Journault's beautiful blue bitch *Am. Can. Ch. Artizoe Color of My Love.* Will and "Adelle" went second in Group at Westminster in 1999.

Will Alexander with Ch. Artizoe Color of My Love
(photo courtesy of Lise Trottier and Louis Journalt — Artizoe)

Laurell Leonard Schneider is the daughter of English Setter breeders Ed and Sharon Leonard (Sir Cedric Kennels). She apprenticed under Mark Threfell and has already piloted top-winning English Setters. Her efforts with *Ch. Brasswinds Sitn' ona Gold Mine* in the mid-1990s announced her presence to the fancy. She continues to move up the ladder of success.

This chapter should be looked at as a mini-chronicle of professional handlers and the development of their talent. While it focuses on English Setters, most of the handlers mentioned were highly successful and talented "all-breed" handlers who were masters of their craft. In the beginning of the modern era of AKC dog shows, the great handlers learned their skills as breeders and kennel managers and passed on their accomplishments through an informal yet highly effective apprenticeship program. The growth and development of the PHA helped to preserve the qualities and abilities required of a successful handler. Even a casual reading of this chapter should make it clear that all of these great handlers studied and honed their art for many years. They learned from the best before them and as judges were quick to recognize those who had mastered the art. The two "rules" cannot be better illustrated:

- 1. Start with a great dog.
- 2. Have a talented handler or owner show the dog.

Endnotes

1.   Marsha Hall Brown, interview, 2002.

2.   Virginia Tuck Hall, interview, 2002.

3.   Davis Tuck, *The Complete English Setter*, 1951.

4.   Dr. Carl Sillman, interview, 2002.

5.   "An Interview with Gordon Parham," *1969 ESAA Annual.*

6.   Corky Vroom, interview, 2002.

7.   Anne Rogers Clark, interview, 2002.

8.   Jane Forsyth, interview, 2002.

9.   Virginia Tuck Hall, interview, 2002.

10.   Jane Forsyth, interview, 2002.

11.   "An Interview with Marge O'Connell," *Setters Inc.*, June/July 1986.

12.   Ibid.

13.   Jane Forsyth, interview, 2002.

14.   Ibid.

15.   Corky Vroom, interview, 2002.

16.   Jane Forsyth, interview, 2002.

17.   Ibid.

Chapter Eleven

The Best of the Best

Ch. Blue Dan of Happy Valley
(portrait photo courtesy of Marsh Hall Brown)

A_{s} this book has documented, English Setters have from the beginning been top show dogs. Since 1924, when the AKC implemented the modern dog show rules, each decade had produced not one but many English Setters that were big winners. English Setters have been dominant at the Group and All-Breed levels and have superbly represented the breed in the Specialty ring. As the reader studies the photos and visualizes the standard, keep in mind that *every dog mentioned in this book was a great example of the breed and one of the top-winning English.* As long as breeders and owners continue to observe the principles handed down by *Laverack, Llewellin, Mallwyd, Crombie, Selkirk, Mallhawk, Happy Valley, Maridor, Delwed, Blue Bar, Silvermine, Rock Falls, Margand, Manlove, Hiddenlane, Clariho, Guys 'n Dolls, Goodtime, Fieldplay, and Set'r Ridge*, the English Setter will always be a top show-winning Sporting dog. In Davis Tuck's book, *The Complete English Setter*, his third chapter is appropriately titled "The Blueprint of The English Setter." The blueprint has not changed, and newer breeders can follow it and his "winning strain" just as Marge O'Connell, Sally Howe, Jane Slosson, Neal Weinstein, Angie Sparkes, the Stevenses, and Melissa Newman all did.

Now it is time to offer my carefully weighed judgment on who were the "best of the best." This short list is by no means cast in stone. It is intended largely to "set the bar" for future English Setter breeders and owners to strive for. A basic fact in the world of show dogs is that no record of achievement will stand indefinitely. Individually, each remains a tribute to the dog that attained it, but the larger purpose is to inspire continued excellence and even greater achievements.

Let's start with the males. Here I must choose *Ch. Rock Falls Colonel, Ch. Blue Dan of Happy Valley, Ch. Sturdy Max, Ch. Maro of Maridor, Ch. Silvermine Wagabond, and Ch. Chandelle's Anchor Man.* Why these? It is not simply their Best in Show records—an all but incredible combined two-hundred-plus; it's the way they earned those records. Two of these dogs were (for a time) the best of all in the AKC. Each of these dogs captured and radiated that spirit that lit up the ring for the English Setter fancier, judge, and spectator alike. They *showed*, they *performed*, with a magnificent grace and beauty that will never be forgotten. Read again what was said about them at the time they were showing. They each represented the breed in the Group and Best rings at the Garden and Morris & Essex. Anchor Man, Blue Dan, and Wagabond won multiple Nationals, while the Colonel and Maro's litter brothers triumphed in the Nationals ring.

Left: Ch. Rock Falls Colonel at 1951 Morris & Essex K.C.
(photo courtesy of St. Hubert's Animal Welfare Center, Madison N.J.)

Ch. Sturdy Max at 1937 Morris & Essex
(photo courtesy of St. Hubert's Animal Welfare Center, Madison N.J.)

*Ch. Maro of Maridor
(photo courtesy of St. Hubert's
Animal Welfare Center,
Madison N.J.)*

*Ch. Silvermine Wagabond
(photo courtesy Virginia
Tuck Hall)*

*Ch. Chandelle's Anchor
Man
(photo from archives of
Marsha Hall Brown)*

Now for the bitches. Here I have picked six that stand out from the rest. They are *Ch. Goodtime's Silk Teddy, Ch. Guys 'n Dolls Annie O'Brien, Ch. Canberra's Legend, Ch. Reidwood Poetry in Motion, Ch. Set'r Ridges Wyndswept in Gold, and Ch. Honeygait N Lampliter Fever.* With more than 100 BIS and 70 BISS, these beautiful bitches proved that the Best in Show ring and even more emphatically the National Specialty rings were not exclusively male provinces. Together, these bitches won 8 National Specialties—more than Anchor Man, Blue Dan, Wagabond, the Colonel, Maro, Daro, and Racket combined! Each broke new ground for English Setter bitches, and each was wonderful to behold.

Ch. Goodtime's Silk Teddy
(photo courtesy Craig & Angie Sparkes-Goodtime)

Ch. Canberra's Legend
            (photo from archives of Marsha Hall Brown)

Ch. Guys 'n Dolls Annie O'Brien
            (photo courtesy of Garth Gourlay archives)

Ch. Reidwood Poetry in Motion
(photo courtesy of Nancy Warner)

Ch. Honeygait Lampliter N Fever
(photo courtesy of David & Judy Mates - Lampliter)

Now for the breeders. The unquestioned giant among English Setter breeders is *Clinton N. Myers.* His *Blue Bar* kennels produced more than 125 Blue Bar champions—and that counts only the champions bred and owned by Mr. Myers. No complete record exists of the many other champions that were sired by his Blue Bar dogs. He owned eight ESAA National Specialty winners and was the person most responsible for preserving the Mallwyd line that Davis Tuck and James Haring define as the "winning strain." Blue Bar dogs were vital to the great breeding programs of my next choice, *Marge O'Connell's Ben-Dar* and *Hiddenlane* lines. Initially with her Ben-Dar kennels and later through her Hiddenlane Kennels, Marge ensured that the "winning strain" found in Blue Bar and Davis Tuck's Silvermine lines was continued. Her influence on English Setter stock, particularly in the Midwest, is felt to this day. The next breeder on my list of greats is *Neal Weinstein.* After a decade (the 1960s) of sons and grandsons of the Colonel and the Blue Bar dogs, Neal strengthened the line and made an indelible mark on the breed with the *Guys 'n Dolls* "spirit." Guys 'n Dolls had robust stud dogs (Shalimar Duke, Onassis, and Barrister Beau) and beautiful bitches that not only won but also produced many top-winning English. Honorable mention must be made to *Sally and Dick Howe's* and *Jane Slosson's Clariho Kennels.* They preserved the beauty and head-pieces of the classic English Setter by melding the Northeast kennels of Stone Gables, Meadboro, and Skidby with the winning strain. *Colonel and Mrs. Robert Stevens' Fieldplay Kennels* and *Melissa Newman's Set'r Ridge Kennels* round out the list. As mentioned earlier, Fieldplay has produced, and continues to produce, remarkable stock that was used in the breeding of many of the top English Setters of the last twenty years. They are keepers of the "winning strain." Set'r Ridge has had a truly remarkable record of accomplishments. Starting with Ch. Fieldplay's Set'r Ridge Jahil, a foundation male bred by Colonel and Mrs. Stevens out of their National Specialty-winning bitch Ch. Windem's Lotsa Dots (from a strong Clariho line) and Ch. Guys 'n Dolls Barrister Beau (an Annie O'Brien son), Set'r Ridge Kennels has produced more than 20 BIS winners (seventeen sired by Hadji) and 4 National Specialty winners. In the decade of the '90s, this kennel's impact on the breed was profound.

Left: C.N. Myers with Ch. Rip of Blue Bar (photo courtesy of Dr. Carl Sillman, ESAA Historian)

Middle: Marge O'Connell (photo from author's collection)

Bottom: Neal Weinstein (photo from archives of Marsha Hall Brown)

Top: Sally & Richard Howe (photos from archives of Marsha Hall Brown)

Col. Robert & Frances Stevens (photo courtesy of Col. Robert & Frances Stevens – Fieldplay)

Melissa Newman (photo courtesy of Melissa Newman – Set'r Ridge)

Finally, the handlers. When you look at the total impact a handler has had on the great Setters and more, one name stands out—*Jane Kamp Forsyth*. This remarkable and talented woman was not only a great handler (certainly one of the best all-breed handlers ever), but she (and her husband Bob) had significant influence on all subsequent handlers. Of the ten handlers I mentioned after the write-up on Jane and Bob Forsyth (in Chapter 10), eight were directly or indirectly tutored, trained, or influenced by Jane Forsyth. And as a judge, her influence on handlers and English Setter breeders and owners is beyond measure. Renowned for her "eye," Jane has had an enduring effect on all who have shown under her (both professionals and breeder-owners). Her talent and skills with Setters, together with her remarkable ability to teach those skills and her influence through a long and illustrious judging career, make her the paradigm of the English Setter handler.

Jane Kamp with Ch. Rock Falls Racket
(photo courtesy of Garth Gourlay archives)

All of the data and facts in this book can be reduced to some simple observations. Owners of great English Setters and the great English Setter breeders have always been highly objective. They studied the breed and made decisions that were as unbiased as possible. Competitors bred to each other's stock if it would produce a better Setter. Breeders did not confine their activities to local areas. From the earliest days of English Setters in America, breeders went from coast to coast to match dogs and continue producing quality Setters.[1] If this book proves nothing else, it shows that color has little to do with winning. ***But markings matter.*** None of the great oranges, blues, and tris in this book were mis-marked or patched or overly roan. Their markings had to be pleasing to the eye, for ***English Setters are meant to be beautiful!***

The Appendixes present a full list of all the great English Setters and their accomplishments. After more than twenty-five years in English Setters and fifteen years spent on the research that went into this book, I have developed a deep love and affection for English Setters and an awe for what great show dogs they are.

The great dogs all had three things in common. First, they were beautiful examples of breed type with wonderful coloration and markings. Second, they were handled by owners or professionals who were masters of their craft. Third, they had a desire to perform and love of the show ring that they communicated to those showing, watching, and judging. It takes all three to have a great dog. You need type and beauty; you need heart and soul; and you need to present these magnificent creatures in their full glory. And to do this last part, you need to become a master handler. One of the lists in the Appendixes is for those English Setters winning three or more Specialties in a career. Overwhelmingly, they were owner-handled. Those owners who became students of the breed are on a par with the best professional handlers, and often they are better than most handlers. Study the masters—both owners and professionals.

The following article from the May 1956 issue of *Popular Dogs* was written by Bill Holt, owner and handler of the incomparable Ch. Rock Falls Colonel. It is by far the best description I know of the heart and soul of great English Setters. As you read this, think of all the great Setters, and especially those that you may have owned and shown. Their indefinable spirit and heart, shared by all English Setters, is the "magic" that captures our hearts.

Long will I remember and never will I forget this great dog and the art of living he has so patiently tried to teach me. Colonel no doubt has an insight on life which he would be happy to convey to every other living creature, and if we as humans could follow his lead, then I am sure we would not only find happiness ourselves but in turn would convey it to our fellow human beings.

Colonel was a lost dog when—after years of campaigning with the spirit that never said die—he found himself for almost a year not being called upon or allowed to take part in the sport for which he was so well adapted. It was Colonel who took me to Westminster [in 1956 at age eight] and there again confirmed my conviction that greats are great because they ARE GREAT and do their bit in this world not for personal gain or reward but because they are Great. He walked into Madison Square Garden with not one thought of leaning for a moment on the many honors which have been so generously bestowed on him by his many, many friends but to confirm again and justify their faith and good wishes.

Surely in the wisdom of this great dog, he must have known I did not need to be assured, but before he entered the ring, just as a precaution, he looked up at me and no plainer words have ever been spoken than when he said, "The time is now and I am ready." Certainly from that moment he never faltered even though the floor was slick and the night was hot. It was the heart of the great, driving on, giving his all to the bitter end. When it was all over, and I took him to his crate, for the first time in his life before going in, he turned and in his most gentle way, lifted his front paws, planting them firmly on my shoulders and stood there momentarily without an eye or muscle moving, then dropped to the floor and went immediately in. I do believe he said, "We have no apologies, we gave our all [a first in Group win] *and we sincerely hope the winner is as happy as we would have been.*

Bill & Tillie Holt with Ch. Rock Falls Colonel
(photo from archives of Bill and Lovey Trotter- Flecka's)

The BIS winner that day was Toy Poodle Ch. Wilber White Swan, handled by none other than Anne Hone Rogers (Clark) winning her first of 3 BIS at the Garden—the best should always be competing against the best.

My sincere hope is that this work will inspire English Setter breeders, owners, and newcomers to the breed to continue the traditions of the great Setters we have seen. Best in Show awards and Best in Specialty Show awards are accomplishments never forgotten. Whether your Setter wins one or one hundred Best in Shows, the joy and excitement of the moment will last forever. To those whose dogs have been mentioned and to the people who helped them excel, congratulations on your accomplishments. To those to come, welcome!

C. S. S., 2002

Endnotes

1. Prior to the advent of jet airliners, breeders sent dogs by rail between distant areas of the United States and Canada. Railway Express, a major shipping company, handled most of the dogs shipped between coasts.

Appendixes

- **Appendix A: Official Standard of the English Setter**
- **Appendix B: Historical Lists of English Setter Achievements**

Appendix B contains data tables[1] of the English Setters selected for mention in this book. The following tables are presented:

Table 1: Lists of English Setter "Firsts" and Records

Table 2: Top-Winning English Setters: Ranked by AKC All-Breed Best in Show Wins (five or more BIS through 2002)

Table 3: Top-Winning English Setters: Ranked by Number of Best of Breeds at English Setter Specialty Shows, 1954-2002 (three or more BISS)

Table 4: ESAA National Specialty Best of Breed Winners, 1932-2002

Table 5: English Setter Association of America Futurity Winners, 1936-2002

Table 6: ESAA Combined Setter Specialty Winners, 1960-2001

Table 7: Westminster KC and Morris & Essex KC Group and BIS English Setters, 1924-2002 & 1927-57

Table 8: Top Ten English Setter Sires, Through December 2002

Table 9: Top Ten English Setter Dams, Tthrough December 2002

---

1. These data have been complied from official AKC records accessed in the AKC Library, published in the AKC Gazette *and* AKC Gazette *Awards Issues. Additionally, the author has purchased AKC awards records to verify all data. Every effort has been made to ensure accuracy. If any reader has data that can add to or alter the facts presented in this book, please contact the author or the publisher. Appropriate corrections will be made in future editions.*

Appendix A: Official Standard for the English Setter

General Appearance—an elegant, substantial and symmetrical gun dog suggesting the ideal blend of strength, stamina, grace, and style. Flat-coated with feathering of good length. Gaiting freely and smoothly with long forward reach, strong rear drive and firm topline. Males decidedly masculine without coarseness. Females decidedly feminine without over refinement. Overall appearance, balance, gait, and purpose to be given more emphasis than any component part. Above all, extremes of anything distort type and must be faulted.

Head—Size and proportion in harmony with body. Long and lean with a well-defined stop. When viewed from the side, head planes (top of muzzle, top of skull, and bottom of lower jaw) are parallel. **Skull**—oval when viewed from above, of medium width, without coarseness, and only slightly wider at the earset than at the brow. Moderately defined occipital protuberance. Length of skull from occiput to stop equal in length of muzzle. **Muzzle**—long and square when viewed from the side, of good depth with flews squared and fairly pendant. Width in harmony with width of skull and equal at nose and stop. Level from eyes to tip of nose. **Nose**—black or brown, fully pigmented. Nostrils wide apart and large. **Foreface**—skeletal structure under the eyes well chiseled with no suggestion of fullness. Cheeks present a smooth and clean-cut appearance. **Teeth**—close scissors bite preferred. Even bite acceptable. **Eyes**—dark brown, the darker the better. Bright and spaced to give a mild and intelligent expression. Nearly round, fairly large, neither deepset nor protruding. Eyelid rims dark and fully pigmented. Lids fit tightly so that haw is not exposed. **Ears**—set well back and low, even with or below eye level. When relaxed carried close to the head. Of moderate length, slightly rounded at the ends, moderately thin leather, and covered with silky hair.

Neck and Body—**Neck**—long and graceful, muscular and lean. Arched at the crest and clean-cut where it joins the head at the basis of the skull. Larger and more muscular toward the shoulders, with the base of the neck flowing smoothly into the shoulders. Not too throaty. **Topline**—in motion or standing appears level or sloping slightly downward without swaying or drop from withers to tail forming a graceful outline of medium length. **Forechest**—well developed, point of sternum projecting slightly in front of point of shoulder/upper arm joint. **Chest**—deep, but not so wide or round as to interfere with the action of the forelegs. Brisket deep enough to reach the level of the elbow. **Ribs**—long, springing gradually to the middle of the body, then tapering as they approach the end of the chest cavity. **Back**—straight and strong at its junction with loin. **Loin**—strong, moderate in length, slightly arched. Tuck up moderate. **Hips**—croup nearly flat. Hip bones wide apart, hips rounded and blending smoothly into hind legs. **Tail**—a smooth continuation of the topline. Tapering to a fine point with only sufficient length to reach the hock joint or slightly less. Carried straight and level with the back. Feathering straight and silky, hanging loosely in a fringe.

Forequarters—Shoulders—shoulder blade well laid back. Upper arm equal in length to and forming a nearly right angle with the shoulder blade. Shoulder blades lie flat and meld smoothly with contours of body. **Forelegs**—from front or side, forelegs straight and parallel. Elbows have no tendency to turn in or out when standing or gating. Arm flat and muscular. Bone substantial but not coarse and muscles hard and devoid of flabbiness. **Pasterns**—short, strong and nearly round with the slope deviating very slightly forward from the perpendicular. **Feet**—face directly forward. Toes closely set, strong and well arched. Pads well developed and tough. Dewclaws may be removed.

Hindquarters—Wide, muscular thighs and well developed lower thighs. Pelvis equal in length to and forming a nearly right angle with upper thigh. In balance with forequarter assembly. Stifle well bent and strong. Lower thigh only slightly longer than upper thigh. Hock joint well bent and strong. Rear pastern short, strong, nearly round and perpendicular to the ground. Hind legs, when seen from the rear, straight and parallel to each other. Hock joints have no tendency to turn in or out when standing or gaiting.

Coat—Flat without curl or wooliness. Feathering on ears, chest, abdomen, underside of thighs, back of all legs and on the tail of good length but not so excessive as to hide true lines and movement or to affect the dogs appearance or function as a sporting dog.

Markings and Color—**Markings**—white ground color with intermingling of darker hairs resulting in Belton markings varying in degree from clear distinct flecking to roan shading, but flecked all over preferred. Head and the ear patches acceptable, heavy patches of color on the body undesirable. **Color**—orange Belton, blue Belton (white with black markings), tri-color (blue Belton and with tan on muzzle, over the eyes and on the legs), lemon Belton, liver Belton.

Movement and Carriage—an effortless graceful movement demonstrating endurance while covering ground efficiently. Long forward reach and strong rear drive with a lively tail and a proud head carriage. Head may be carried slightly lower when moving to allow for greater reach of forelegs. The back strong, firm, and free of roll. When moving at a trot, as speed increases, the legs tend to converge toward a line representing the center of gravity.

Size—Dogs about 25 inches; Bitches about 24 inches.

Temperament—Gentle, affectionate, friendly, without shyness, fear, or viciousness.

Approved November 11, 1986

Appendix B

Table 1: Lists of English Setter "Firsts" and Records

First AKC-registered dog, AKC # 1	Adonis –1876
First AKC dog to amass 100 BIS	Ch. Rock Falls Colonel–1949-1955
First English Setter OFA, OFA ES-1	Ch. Merry Rover of Valley Run
First English Setter dual champion	Dual Ch. Heathrow Rainbow Robber CDX–1985
First English Setter National Specialty winner	Ch. Blue Dan of Happy Valley–1932
First English Setter Futurity winner	Stucile's Forever Yours–1936
First **"revived"** ESAA Futurity winner	Ch.Guys 'n Dolls Molly Bloom–1976
First English Setter to win BIS at Morris & Essex KC	Ch. Sturdy Max–1937
First English Setter to win BIS at Westminster KC	Ch. Daro of Maridor–1938
First English Setter Obedience Trail championship	O.T. Ch. Cornell's Queen Princess–1980

English Setter Record Holders

Most AKC Best in Shows–male	Ch. Rock Falls Colonel–*100**
Most AKC Best in Show –female	Ch. Goodtime's Silk Teddy – 39
Most AKC Sporting Group Wins–male	Ch. Rock Falls Colonel –162
Most AKC Sporting Group Wins–female	Ch. Goodtime's Silk Teddy–*163**
Most ESAA National Specialty Best of Breeds (tie–3*)	Ch. Guys 'n Doll's Annie O'Brien– 1974, 1975, 1976 Ch. Goodtime's Silk Teddy– 1988, 1989, 1990
Most English Setter Specialty Best of Breeds–male	Ch. Chandelle's Anchor Man–*23**
Most English Setter Specialty Best of Breeds–female	Ch. Set'r Ridge Wyndswept in Gold–18
Most English Setter Best of Breed wins–male	Ch. Timbertrail's Riptide–*285**
Most English Setter Best of Breed wins–female	Ch. Honeygait N Lampliter Fever–**270**
Most English Setter AKC champions sired	Dual Ch. Set'r Ridge's Solid Gold–*127**
Most-American-titled English Setter	Dual Ch. Set'r Ridge's Solid Gold CDX, MH, HDX, CGC
Most AKC BIS by a one-year-old	Ch. Maro of Maridor—*4**
Most AKC BIS by a two-year-old	Ch. Maro of Maridor—*6**
Most AKC BIS by a blue Belton	Ch. Blue Dan of Happy Valley–24
Most AKC BIS by a tri-color	Ch. Zamitz's Jumpin' Jack–6

* = the absolute AKC English Setter breed record

Other notable English Setter "Firsts"

First rotating ESAA National Specialty   Hosted by Ohio ESC–1968

First litter mates (brother and sister)
   to win ESAA BISS   Ch. Sir Herbert of Kennelworth–1950
                                       Ch. Miss Frivilous–1951
   (by Ch. Rip of Blue Bar x Vivacious Doll Of Vilmar, both owned by C. N. Myers)

First bitch to win an ESAA National BISS   Ch. Deli of Blue Bar–1938

First ES to win 2 ESAA Nationals   Ch. Pilot of Crombie of Happy Valley–
                                       1934 & 1936

First ES to win 2 **consecutive** ESAA
   Nationals   Ch. Daro of Maridor–1940-41

First litter mates (brother and sister)   Ch. Chandelle's Anchor Man–BISS
   to win BISS and BOS at the same   Ch. Chandelle's Bambi–BOS, 1967
   ESAA National Specialty

First father & son to win ESAA Nationals   Ch. Sturdy Max–1937 &
                                       Ch. Daro of Maridor–1940-41

First father & daughter to win ESAA   Ch. Pilot of Crombie of Happy Valley–
   Nationals   1934 & 1936
                                       Ch. Deli of Blue Bar–1939

First mother & daughter to win ESAA   Ch. Lampliter's Atta-Tud O' Trabeiz–
   Nationals   1996-97
                                       Ch. Trabeiz Premonition of a Dream–1999

Table 2: Top-Winning English Setters
Ranked by AKC All-Breed Best in Show Wins
(five or more BIS through 2002)

Rank	Name of Setter	Sex	#BIS	AKC #	Years shown
1	CH. ROCK FALLS COLONEL	M	100	S-329961	1950-55
2	CH. MARO OF MARIDOR	M	55	A-231572	1939-43
3	CH. GOODTIME'S SILK TEDDY	F	39	SE-583667	1988-90
4	CH. HONEYGAIT N LAMPLITER FEVER	F	38	SN-43790101	1999-2003
5	CH. BLUE DAN OF HAPPY VALLEY	M	24	762756	1930-33
6	CH. SIR GUY OF DELWED	M	23	A-278646	1940-45
7	CH. FOXTRACT'S THE INVINCIBLE ONE	M	16	SE-326795	1987-90
8	CH. THE COUNTRY GENTLEMAN	M	14	784230	1932-36
9	CH. TIMBERTRAILS RIPTIDE	M	14	SD-967145	1986-90
10	CH. SET'R RIDGE WYNDSWEPT IN GOLD	F	14		1998-2002
11	CH. GILROYS CHIEF TOPIC	M	13	799765	1932-39
12	CH. STURDY MAX	M	13	944324	1934-37
13	CH. LUDAR OF BLUE BAR	M	13	S-454627	1950-54
14	CH. GUYS'N DOLLS ANNIE O'BRIEN	F	13	SB-18903	1973-76
15	CH. SET'R RIDGE LOOKIN' AT YOU KID	M	13	SM-965689/01	1994-97
16	CH. LORIEN'S FIRE BRIGADE	M	11	SC-936160	1983-87
17	CH. MERRY ROVER OF VALLEY RUN	M	10	SA-116098	1965-68
18	CH. ROBINHOOD OF MARIONAL	M	9	911616	1935-37
19	CH. MODERN BOY OF STUCILE	M	8	A-5015	1938-39
20	CH. PILOT OF CROMBIE OF HAPPY VALL	M	7	881743	1934-37
21	CH. CEDRIC OF DELWED	M	7	A-278647	1939-44
22	CH. RIP OF BLUE BAR	M	7	A-749742	1946-48
23	CH. IKE OF BLUE BAR	M	7	S-586365	1954-57
24	CH. CANDLEWOOD DISTINCTION	M	7	SA-3229	1960-64
25	CH. DRUMMONT'S TASTY'S BILLY	M	7	SC-408484	1980-83
26	CH. ZAMITZ JUMPIN' JACK	M	6	S-800882	1959-60
27	CH. CHANDELLE'S ANCHOR MAN	M	6	SA-95127	1963-70
28	CH. GUYS'N DOLLS SHALIMAR DUKE	M	6	SA-342335	1969-71
29	CH. TIMBERTRAIL'S SIGN OF TRENT	M	6	SF-758685	1992-95
30	CH. COUNTRY SQUIRE LONE STAR	M	6	SN-100861/05	1996-99
31	CH. FRED OF CROMBIE	M	5	655946	1929
32	CH. SIR ORKNEY OF WILLGRESS JR.	M	5	702187	1934-37
33	CH. DARO OF MARIDOR	M	5	A-231570	1938-43
34	CH. BLUE BAR LIMITED	M	5	A-293396	1940
35	CH. DIVE BOMBER	M	5	A-559459	1943-45
36	CH. ROCK FALLS RACKET	M	5	S-254264	1951-54
37	CH. MARGAND LORD BALTIMORE	M	5	S-846454	1959-62
38	CH. BRIARPATCH OF BRYN MAWR	M	5	SA-724673	1973-74
39	CH. FANTAILS SUNSHINE MAN	M	5	SD-025352	1982-84
40	CH. BRASSWINDS SITN ON A GOLDMINE	M	5	SE-537194	1987-93
41	CH. OAKLEY'S CIGAR	M	5	SN-538911/01	1998-2001

Table 3: Top-Winning English Setters Ranked by Number of Best of Breeds at English Setter Specialty Shows: 1954-2002 (three or more BISS)

Rank	Name of Setter	Sex	#BISS	Years shown
1	CH. CHANDELLE'S ANCHOR MAN	M	23	1963-1970
2	CH. SET'R RIDGE WYNDSWEPT IN GOLD	F	18	1998-
3	CH. REIDWOOD POETRY IN MOTION	F	14	1993-1998
4	CH. HONEYGAIT N LAMPLITER FEVER	F	13	1999-
5	CH. SIR KIP OF MANITOU	M	12	1967-1969
6	CH. GOODTIME'S SILK TEDDY	F	11	1988-1990
7	CH. DRUMMONT'S TASTY'S BILLY	M	10	1980-1983
8	CH. BRASSWINDS SIT'N ON A GOLDMINE	M	10	1988-1993
9	CH. KELYRIC CALIFORNIA SUN	M	10	1988-1994
10	CH. GOODTIME ROYALE SALUTE	M	10	1992-1997
11	CH. SET'R RIDGE'S SOLID GOLD	M	10	1988-1998
12	CH. GUYS'N DOLLS ANNIE O'BRIEN	F	9	1973-1976
13	CH. TIMBERTRAILS RIPTIDE	M	9	1986-1991
14	CH. MERRY ROVER OF VALLEY RUN	M	8	1964-1966
15	CH. GUYS'N DOLLS SHALIMAR DUKE	M	8	1968-1971
16	CH. LORIEN'S FIRE BRIGADE	M	8	1983-1987
17	CH. KELYRIC BLUEPRINT	M	8	1983-1987
18	CH. LAMPLITER ATTAH-TUD O'TRABEIZ	F	8	1994-2002
19	CH. FIELDPLAY'S WINDY SKYE	F	8	2000-2002
20	CH. CHATTERWOOD ON THE ROCKS	M	7	1956-1958
21	CH. TIMBERTRAIL'S SIGN OF TRENT	M	7	1992-1996
22	CH. KELYRIC JELLY'S LAST JAM	M	7	1995-1998
23	CH. TRABEIZ PREMONITION OF A DREAM	B	7	1996-1999
24	CH. HONEYGAIT GOODTIME HOT TOPIC	M	7	1998-2000
25	CH. CANDLEWOOD DISTINCTION	M	6	1961-1965
26	CH. FLECKA'S FLASH OF CABIN HILL	M	6	1962-1964
27	CH. CANBERRA'S LEGEND	F	6	1968-1970
28	CH. GUYS'N DOLLS TASTE OF HONEY	F	6	1976-1979
29	CH. FOXTRACT'S THE INVINCIBLE ONE	M	6	1987-1990
30	CH. WILLGLEN LIBERTY CELEBRATION	F	6	1988-1991
31	CH. HEATHROW'S A CASE OF BLACKMALE	M	6	1988-1991
32	CH. OAKLEY'S CIGAR	M	6	2000-2001
33	CH. ESTHETES SPENDOR IN THE GRASS	M	6	2000-2002
34	CH. ZAMITZ JUMPIN' JACK	M	5	1959-1962
35	CH. FLECKA'S CHARLIE	M	5	1960-1962
36	CH. GUYS'N DOLLS ROSA MIDNIGHT	F	5	1973-1977
37	CH. HIDDENLANE'S BENCHMARK	M	5	1973-1976
38	CH. HIDDENLANE SPECIAL DELIVERY	F	5	1977-1980
39	CH. VELVETS BLUE MOON	M	5	1978-1981
40	CH. HEMLOCK LANE-O'LAWDY'S TIME OUT	F	5	1984-1990

Rank	Name of Setter	Sex	#BISS	Years shown
41	CH. MARKSMAN'S WINTERIDGE LEGEND	M	5	1989-1991
42	CH. COLUMBINE SILKEN SKY	F	5	1990-1994
43	CH. BRASSWINDS CINNAMON SUGAR	F	5	1993-1995
44	CH. SET'R RIDGE LOOKIN AT YOU KID	M	5	1993-1996
45	CH. ESTHETE'S MADAME X	F	5	1995-1998
46	CH. ARTIZOE NELSON CASANOVA	M	5	1997-1999
47	CH.TRABEIZ PREMIER ELEMENT OF SUPRISE	M	5	1999-2001
48	CH. MARGAND LORD BALTIMORE	M	4	1959-1961
49	CH. GUYLINE'S FLYING TIGER	M	4	1971-1972
50	CH. GUYS'N DOLLS ONASSIS	M	4	1971-1974
51	CH. BURR RIDGE CONSTELLATION	F	4	1976-1977
52	CH. FIVE OAKES PISTOL PETE	M	4	1977-1984
53	CH. LORIEN'S AMERICAN FLYER	M	4	1979-1982
54	CH. BRICKTON REAU'S HIGH TIDE	M	4	1980-1983
55	CH. WINDEM'S LOTSA DOTS	F	4	1983-1986
56	CH. WILLGLEN MAJOR MOTION	M	4	1987-1989
57	CH. REIDWOOD SYMPHONY IN MOTION	F	4	2000-2002
58	CH. COUNTRY SQUIRE LONE STAR	M	3	1996-1998
59	CH. ENGLISH ACCENT OF VALLEY RUN	M	3	1960-1961
60	CH. BAKER'S NORTHERN LANCER	M	3	1968-1969
61	CH. HIDDENLANE'S MERRY MAX	M	3	1970-1974
62	CH. HIGHLAND'S WHIP OF PENMAEN	M	3	1971-1973
63	CH. CLARIHO KRISTOFER OF CRIT-DO	M	3	1972-1974
64	CH. CHARLIN RUDOLPH	M	3	1973-1978
65	CH. ARUNDEL'S DUKE OF NORFOLK	M	3	1973-1975
66	CH. STORYBOOKS BEST SELLER	M	3	1976-1978
67	CH. CLARIHO KNIGHT RIDER	M	3	1977
68	CH. GARSON'S SPECIAL PROSECUTOR	M	3	1979-1984
69	CH. MYSTIS TRIUMPH OF VALLEY RUN	M	3	1981-1984
70	CH. WILEIRE HOLLY GO LIGHTLY	F	3	1983-1985
71	CH. GOODTIME GLORY ROSEBUD	F	3	1985-1986
72	CH. NEVERDONE'S FIVE OAKES VICTOR	M	3	1985-1989
73	CH. SEAL ROCK'S ENGLISH TRIFLE	M	3	1986-1988
74	CH. COUNTRY SQUIRE LUCKY STAR	M	3	1988-1992
75	CH. FIELDPLAY'S ABE LINCOLN	M	3	1990-1994
76	CH. WINDEM'S SPEAK OF THE DEVIL	M	3	1993-1995
77	CH. SET'R RIDGE'S BLUEPRINT ZABRI	F	3	1993-1996
78	CH. CAROB PAINTED ON JEANS	M	3	1993-1998
79	CH. REIDWOOD'S DARE TO DREAM	M	3	1994-1996
80	CH. GOLD RUSH FANCY DANCER	F	3	1995-1996
81	CH. MARKSMAN BURR RIDGE BOND	M	3	1997-1999
82	CH. BROOKLIN DRIFTWIND DREAMQUEST	M	3	1999-2002
83	CH. INDIANBEND HOT ITEM OF PAMIR	M	3	2001-2002
84	CH. REIDWOOD ARTISTRY IN MOTION	M	3	2001-2002
85	CH. SUNSHINE PALACE S. GOLDEN STATE	M	3	2001-2002

Table 4: ESAA National Specialty Best of Breed Winners—1932-2002

Year	Name of Setter	Year	Name of Setter
1932	Ch. Blue Dan of Happy Valley	1968	Ch. Sir Kip of Manitou
1933	The Country Gentleman	1969	Ch. Sir Kip of Manitou
1934	Ch. Pilot of Crombie of Happy Valley	1970	Ch. Guys 'n Dolls Shalimar Duke
1935	Ch. Robin Hood of Marional	1971	Ch. Hiddenlane's Merry Max
1936	Ch. Pilot of Crombie of Happy Valley	1972	Ch. Sukarlas Sandpiper
1937	Ch. Sturdy Max	1973	Ch. Hiddenlane's Benchmark
1938	Ch. Lakewoods Yuba	1974	Ch. Guys 'n Dolls Annie O'Brien
1939	Ch. Deli of Blue Bar	1975	Ch. Guys 'n Dolls Annie O'Brien
1940	Ch. Daro of Maridor	1976	Ch. Guys 'n Dolls Annie O'Brien
1941	Ch. Daro of Maridor	1977	Ch. Sunburst Special Edition
1942	Ch. Big Boy of Rockboro	1978	Ch. Storybooks Best Seller
1943	Ch. Lem of Blue Bar	1979	Ch. Velvets Blue Moon
1944	Ch. Prune's Own Maxson's Dawn	1980	Ch. Guys 'n Dolls Molly Bloom
1945	Ch. Rip of Blue Bar	1981	Ch. Dummonts Tasty Billy
1946	Ch. Prune's Own Palmer	1982	Ch. Ebtides Me and My Shadow
1947	Ch. Rip of Blue Bar	1983	Ch. Windems Lotsa Dots
1948	Ch. Silvermine Wagabond	1984	Ch. Fantails Sunshine Man
1949	Ch. Silvermine Wagabond	1985	Ch. Neverdone Five Oaks Victor
1950	Ch. Herbert of Kennelworth	1986	Ch. Stagedoor Abbyroad
1951	Ch. Miss Frivolous	1987	Ch. Lorien's Fire Brigade
1952	Ch. Silvermine Whipcord	1988	Ch. Goodtime's Silk Teddy
1953	Ch. Rock Falls Sky Way	1989	Ch. Goodtime's Silk Teddy
1954	Ch. Rockfalls Racket	1990	Ch. Goodtime's Silk Teddy
1955	Ch. Ike of Blue Bar	1991	Ch. Esquire's Blizzard of Carob
1956	Ch. Ike of Blue Bar	1992	Ch. Ash Hollow's Why Stop Now
1957	Ch. Chatterwood on the Rocks	1993	Ch. Set'r Ridge's Solid Gold
1958	Ch. Chatterwood on the Rocks	1994	Ch. Kelyric California Sun
1959	Ch. Zamitz Jumping Jack	1995	Ch. Carob Painted on Jeans
1960	Ch. Skidby's Sturdy Tyke	1996	Ch. Lampliter Attah-Tud O'Trabeiz
1961	Ch. English Accent of Valley Run	1997	Ch. Lampliter Attah-Tud O'Trabeiz
1962	Ch. Flecka's Flash of Cabin Hill	1998	Ch. Reidwood Poetry in Motion
1963	Ch. Candlewood Distinction	1999	Ch. Trabeiz Premonition of a Dream
1964	Ch. Flecka's Flash of Cabin Hill	2000	Ch. Brasswinds Sonrise Ahhmen
1965	Ch. Candlewood Distinction	2001	Ch. Oakley's Cigar
1966	Ch. Merry Rover of Valley Run	2002	Ch. Set'r Ridges Wyndswept in Gold
1967	Ch. Chandelle's Anchor Man	2003	

Table 5: English Setter Association of America Futurity Winners—1936-2002

Year	Best in Futurity	Best of Opposite Sex in Futurity
1936	Stucile's Forever Yours	
1937	Ch. Appie of Blue Bar	
1938	Maro of Maridor	
1939	Kinsland Soubrette	
1940	Scandal of Shotover	
1941	Ch. Jesse of Blue Bar	
1942	Prune's Own Inherit	
1943	Commando of Hadceda	
1944-75	*No Futurity held*	
1976	Ch. Guys 'n Dolls Molly Bloom	Storybooks Magnum Force
1977	Storybook's Enchancement II	Gold Rush Gold Miner Blues
1978	Matoman's Artemis of Seafield	Erinshire Spark 'em Up
1979	Drummont's Tasty's Billy	Belton Bay's Charmaine
1980	Birchwood's Justin Time	Tattershall n Timbertrail Too
1981	Marksman's Bouquet	Lorien's Fire Cracker
1982	Guys 'n Dolls Miss Billie Perry	Can. Ch. Windem's Fast Forgetting
1983	Indian Bend Color Me Rainbow	Briarstone's Winchester
1984	Guys 'n Dolls Taffeta O'Neal	Guys 'n Dolls Raffles O'Neal
1985	Patchwork Range Rider	Ch. Canberra Editions Soft Touch
1986	Five Oakes Artemis	Foxtract's The Invincible One
1987	Heathrow's Justin O'Sagramore	Silverline Magic Spirit
1988	Ch. Set'r Ridge's Solid Gold	Chebaco's Miss Micha O'Hara
1989	Can. Ch. Artizoe Bonnie LouLou	Can. Ch. Artizoe Beau Bleu
1990	Fieldstone's Brasswind Decoy	Brasswinds Cinnamon Sugar
1991	Chebaco Miss Hedda Hopper	Ch. Sir Cedric's Count Monroe
1992	Ch. Carob Painted on Jeans	Sunburst Ricochet
1993	Stagedoor Run for the Roses	Reidwood Dare to Dream
1994	Maldawn Semalina Satin Jammys	Canberra Guns and Roses
1995	Flower of Lonesome Lane	Stoneyfield's Robin Yount
1996	Somerset Tripoley	Lynann's Fanchon Shining Moments
1997	Set'r Ridge Wyndswept in Gold	Rockmors Dream Catcher
1998	Reidwood Symphony in Motion	Honeygait Goodtime Hot Topic
1999	Brasswinds Sonrise Ahhmen	Heathrow's Bird'N of Proof
2000	Set'r Ridge's Special Effects	Colthouse Millennium Man
2001	Set'r Ridge's Vision	Premier Trabeiz Go Ballistic
2002	Honeygait Wilsonlake Absolut	Pemberley Kiss It Goodbye

Table 6: English Setter Association of America Combined Setter Specialty Winners, 1960-2001

Year	BISS WINNER	Year	BISS WINNER
1960	CH. SKIBY'S STURDY TYKE	1980	TRISTAN OF SPRINGHILL
1961	CH. ENGLISH ACCENT OF VALLEY RUN	1981	CH. CLARIHO BASIL OF STILLWOOD
1962	CH. FLECKA'S FLASH OF CABIN HILL	1982	CH. BRICKTON REAU'S HIGH TIDE
1963	CH.CANDELWOOD DISTINCTION	1983	CH. LORIEN'S FIRE BRIGADE
1964	CH. FLECKA'S FLASH OF CABIN HILL	1984	CH. GARSON'S SPECIAL PROSECUTOR
1965	CH. CANDELWOOD DISTINCTION	1985	CH. KELYRIC'S BLUEPRINT
1966	CH. MERRY ROVER OF VALLEY RUN	1986	CH. WICKETT BUCKHANNON
1967	CH. CHANDELL'S ANCHOR MAN	1987	CH. FOXTRACT'S THE INVINCIBLE ONE
1968	CH. CHANDELL'S ANCHOR MAN	1988	CH. FIELDPLAY'S CAN'T STOP ME NOW
1969	CH. SIR KIP OF MANITOU	1989	CH. GOODTIME SILK TEDDY
1970	CH. GUYS 'N DOLLS SHALIMAR DUKE	1990	CH. TIMBERTRAILS RIPTIDE
1971	CH. GUYLINE FLYING TIGER	1991	BANNERRUN'S SUN MAGIC
1972	CH. CLARIHO KRISTOFFER OFCRITT-DU	1992	CH. KELYRIC CALIFORNIA SUN
1973	CH. GUYS 'N DOLLS ANNIE O'BRIEN	1993	CH. BANNERRUN'S SUN MAGIC
1974	CH. GUYS 'N DOLLS ANNIE O'BRIEN	1994	CH. COLUMBINE'S SILKEN SKY
1975	CH. HIDDENLANE'S BENCHMARK	1995	CH. BRASSWINDS CINNAMON SUGAR
1976	CH. GUYS 'N DOLLS BIG BUTCH	1996	CH. SET'R RIDGE LOOKIN AT YOU KID
1977	CH. GUYS 'N DOLLS TASTE OF HONEY	1997	CH. FLOWER OF LONSOME LANE
1978	CH. CHARLIN RUDOLPH	1998	CH. COUNTRY SQUIRE LONE STAR
1979	CH. TATTERSHALL TAPESTRY	1999	CH. TRABIEZ PREMONITION OF A DREAM
		2000	CH. SET'R RIDGE WYNDSWEPT IN GOLD
		2001	CH. HONEYGAIT N LAMPLITER FEVER

Notes:

1. From 1960 through 1967, the Combined was the ESAA National. In 1968 it became a separate show.
2. The last Combined Setter Specialty was in 2001. It has been replaced with the new Garden Specialty.

Table 7: Westminster KC Group & BIS English Setters, 1924-2002

1931–Ch. Blue Dan of Happy Valley–**Group I**
1932–Ch. Blue Dan of Happy Valley– Group II
1933–Ch. Blue Dan of Happy Valley–**Group I**
1935–Ch. Pilot of Crombie of Happy Valley–Group II
1936–Ch. Pilot of Crombie of Happy Valley–Group III
1937–Ch. Pilot of Crombie of Happy Valley–Group II
1938–Ch. Daro of Maridor–**Group I & BIS**
1940–Ch. Maro of Maridor–Group III
1941–Ch. Maro of Maridor–Group II
1942–Ch. Daro of Maridor–Group II
1943–Ch. Maro of Maridor–Group II
1944–Ch. Daro of Maridor–Group IV
1945–Ch. End O'Maine Sorry–Group III
1946–Ch. Prune's Own Palmer–**Group I**
1948–Ch. Silvermine Wagabond–Group III
1952–Ch. Rock Falls Colonel–**Group I**
1953–Ch. Silvermine Messenger–Group IV
1954–Ch. Mike of Meadboro–Group III
1956–Ch. Rock Falls Colonel–**Group I**
1964–Ch. Candlewood Distinction–Group II
1965–Ch. Candlewood Distinction–Group III
1966–Ch. Merry Rover of Valley Run–Group II
1967–Ch. Merry Rover of Valley Run–Group III
1970–Ch. Shalimar Duke–Group III
1982–Ch. Drummont's Tasty's Billy–**Group I**
1989–Ch. Goodtime's Silk Teddy–Group III
1992–Ch. Brasswind's Sit'n on a Goldmine–Group III
1998–Ch. Artizoe's Color of My Love–Group II

Morris & Essex KC Group & BIS English Setters, 1927-57

1930–Ch. Inglehurst Reward–**Group I**
1931–Ch. Blue Dan of Happy Valley–Group II
1932–Ch. Blue Dan of Happy Valley–Group II
1937–Ch. Sturdy Max–**Group I & BIS**
1938–Ch. Maro of Maridor–**Group I**
1939–Ch. Maro of Maridor–Group III
1940–Ch. Maro of Maridor–**Group I**
1949–Ch. Mary of Blue Bar–Group III
1950–Ch. Sir Herbert of Kennelworth–Group II
1951–Ch. Rock Falls Colonel–**Group I & BIS**
1952–Silvermine Messenger–Group III (from the classes)
1953–Ch. Rock Falls Skyway–**Group I**
1957–Ch. Chatterwood on the Rocks–Group II

Table 8: Top Ten English Setter Sires
(based on number of AKC-registered champion get as of December 2002)

1. **DC Can. Ch. Set'r Ridge's Solid Gold CDX MH HDX CGC (127)**
   By: Am./Can. Ch. Fieldplay's Set'r Ridge Jhahil CD
   Ex: Can. Ch. Bludawns Just Call Me Jenny

2. **Am./Can./Mex. Ch. Gold Rush Gold Miner Blues (89)**
   By: Ch. Clariho War Paint
   Ex: Ch. Guyline's Artemis Of Cymbria

3. **Ch. Guys 'N Dolls Shalimar Duke (76)**
   By: Am./Can. Ch. Hillsdale Sentinel
   Ex: Ch. Guys 'N Dolls Bridget O'Shea CD

4. **Am./Can. Ch. Fieldplay's Set'r Ridge Jhahil CD JH (76)**
   By: Ch. Guys 'N Dolls Barrister Beau
   Ex: Am./Can. Ch. Windem's Lotsa Dots

5. **Ch. Guys 'N Dolls Barrister Beau (74)**
   By: Ch. Seamrog Tyson Of Palomar
   Ex: Ch. Guys 'N Dolls Annie O'Brien

6. **Ch. Guys 'N Dolls Onassis (60)**
   By: Ch. Guys 'N Dolls Shalimar Duke
   Ex: Ch. Lady Dana Of Ellendale

7. **Am./Can. Ch. Five Oakes Pistol Pete (50)**
   By: Ch. Canberra's Flagmaster
   Ex: Am./Can. Ch. Five Oakes Snow Flake

8. **Ch. Windems Speak Of the Devil (48)**
   By: Am./Can. Ch. Fieldplay's Set'r Ridge Jhahil CD JH
   Ex: Ch. Windems Devils Advocate

9. **Ch. Seamrog Tyson Of Palomar (45)**
   By: Ch. Arnee's Nell'Son Of Nor'Coaster
   Ex: Ch. Guys 'N Dolls Ziegfield Girl CD

10. **Am./Can./Ber. Ch. Sir Kip Of Manitou (41)**
    By: Ch. Skidby's Bosun Of Stone Gables
    Ex: High-Tor's Spicy Lady

Table 9: Top Ten English Setter Dams

(based on number of AKC-registered champion get as of December 2002)

1. **Kadons Smart 'N Sassy (26)**
   By: Am./Can. Ch. Windem's Sarad Of Whitehouse
   Ex: Ch. Kadons Flying High

2. **Ch. English Time's Bella Donna (20)**
   By: Am./Can. Ch. Penmaen Back Woodsman
   Ex: Ch. Garson's Sweet Talkin' Woman

3. **Ch. Sunburst Black Magic (20)**
   By: Am./Can./Mex. Ch. Gold Rush Gold Miner Blues
   Ex: Ch. Sunburst Black Velvet

4. **Ch. Foxtract Driving Miss Daisy (18)**
   By: Am./Can. Ch. Gentry Double Trouble
   Ex: Am./Can. Ch. Foxtract's Bewitched

5. **Ch. Solheim's Ginger Snap (17)**
   By: Ch. Guys 'N Dolls Society Max
   Ex: Am./Can. Ch. Fivesmith's Heidi

6. **Ch. Willglen's Vanilla Pudding (17)**
   By: Ch. Willglen's Exciter
   Ex: Ch. Willglen's Elusive Echo

7. **Am./Can. Ch. Windem's Lotsa Dots (17)**
   By: Am./Can. Ch. Windem's Sarad Of Whitehouse
   Ex: Ch. Kadons Flying High

8. **Ch. Checkmate's Sorceress (17)**
   By: Ch. Canberra's Advocate
   Ex: Am./Can. Ch. Oldwick's Bewitched

9. **Ch. Thenderin Golden Dream (16)**
   By: Ch. Thenderin Friar Of Chiltern
   Ex: Autumaura Christmas Debut

10. **Ch. Fieldplay's Dot's Amore (15)**
    By: Ch. Seafield's Holiday Spirit
    Ex: Am./Can. Ch. Windem's Lotsa Dots

Bibliography

The American Kennel Club Blue Book of Dogs, 1938. Garden City Publishing, 1938.

The American Kennel Club Gazette. The American Kennel Club, 1933-2002.

The Complete Dog Book: An Official Publication of the American Kennel Club. Revised edition. Doubleday & Company, 1968.

Brown, Marsha Hall. Interview. December, 2001.

Brown, Marsha Hall. *The Essence of Setters.* Doral Publishing, 2002.

Dog World. Judy Publishing Co., October 1951.

Dogs in Review. Paul Lepiane and Bo Bengtson, publishers, February 2000 and August 2001.

English Setter Association of America Annuals. ESAA, 1945-2001.

English Setter Association of America. Booklet, 1954.

English Setter Association of America. *Official Standard for the English Setter.* Approved November 11, 1986

Fletcher, Walter R. *My Times With Dogs.* Howell Book House, 1980

Forsyth, Jane Kamp. Interview. April, 2002.

Forsyth, Robert. Interview. April, 2002.

Hall, Virginia Tuck Nichols. Interview. March, 2002.

Kessler, Jane R. *The Champion English Setter Index.* Cymbria Setters, 1977.

Laverick, Edward. *The Setter.* England: Longmans, Green, and Co., 1872.

Lloyd, Freeman. *All Setters.* Freeman Lloyd Publishing, 1937.

Maxwell, C. Bede. *The Truth About Sporting Dogs.* Howell Book House, 1972.

The New York Times, February 14, 1951.

Popular Dogs Magazine. Popular Dogs Publishing Company, George F. Foley, publisher, 1935-72.

The Setter Quarterly. Holflin Publishing, summer 1981 and summer 1982.

Setters, Inc. Paul Lepiane and Bo Bengtson, publishers, August/September 1985, June/July 1986, February/March 1988.

Setters, Incorporated. Michael Allen, publisher, winter 1978.

The Sporting Life. Group Publications, December 1992.

Sports Illustrated, February 27, 1956.

Trotter, Mr. & Mrs. William. Interview. December, 2001.

Tuck, Davis. *The Complete English Setter.* Denlinger's, 1951.

Tuck, Davis, and Elsworth Howell. *The New Complete English Setter.* Second edition. Howell Book House, 1964.

Tuck, Davis, and Elsworth Howell. *The New Complete English Setter.* Third edition. Howell Book House, 1972.

Tuck, Davis, Elsworth Howell, and Judy Graef. *The New Complete English Setter.* Fourth edition. Howell Book House, 1982.

Vroom, Corky. Interview. February, 2002.

Index

This book and other fine books from Doral Publishing are available through:

- 4-M Enterprises
- Direct Book Service
- Cherrybrook
- J-B Wholesale
- Drs. Foster & Smith
- Care-A-Lot Pet Supplies
- Jemar Pet Supplies